MUSIC, MAGIC, AND NLP

Unleash your creativity.
change the world

VIC HYLAND

Testimonials

"I started having lessons with Vic from the age of eight until I went to the Brit School at the age of 16, and in that time, I built my technique and knowledge of the instrument, songwriting, and performance. He encouraged me to gig with him from an early age, and we also did seminars and lectures for the RGT in places like the London Guitar Show, which was fun.

I have made a successful career in music because of Vic. Life would have been very different without those lessons!"

Ben Thomas, guitarist (works with Adele and Sam Smith)

"Vic played a pivotal part in my early guitar education, teaching me the foundations initially and then building up through the grades. Every lesson was engaging and interesting, with real relevance to current music. I reached the point where I started to take a real interest in songwriting, and Vic then taught me invaluable techniques and structures to really advance my skills. Above all, I enjoyed my time with Vic and highly recommend him as a teacher. He is an awesome dude!"

Fred Clark, singer-songwriter

"Vic is one hell of a brilliant guitar teacher. For adults and children alike. Really patient, encouraging and highly skilful. Thoroughly recommended! Vic's lessons gave me the confidence and ability to work as a professional actor and musician these last 14 years. I'm currently rocking out in The School of Rock, and in my guitar solo, I use a riff that Vic taught me every show."

Alex Tomkins, West End actor-musician
(School of Rock, The Commitments)

"'If you want to burn, you've got to learn!' Vic is simply the master, not just on his trusty Fender Stratocaster. I owe so much to Vic and continue to be very grateful to him. When I first started out playing for a living, it was very tricky, and it still is! I still seek Vic's guidance and help in becoming a musician. One of the many qualities Vic has is the fact he is a visionary; he has the key to seeing the potential in people and helping in situations that they are in. I, and many others, would not have had the drive or confidence to be a teacher or the player I am if I had not had the opportunities through meeting Vic. Whether you want some recording sessions, lessons, or a gig, go and be a seeker and go and see Vic for yourself. You never know what you may find. We were recently playing at a gig, and after the gig, Vic said, 'That was great.' The truth is, it always is with Vic. Cheers, Vic, for being an inspiration and all that you are."

Grant Tunbridge, musician and teacher

"One of the best music teachers I know. Vic is a great organiser - notably, the annual Blues Camp weekend. He is also a great ambassador for educating children and adults in the many different styles of music, offering support and encouragement. It is a pleasure to work with him."

Sam Kelly, drummer

"I've attended several of Vic Hyland's training courses and seminars. The latest was 'NLP for Music', a one-day course. Anyone who has tried to get through one of the many NLP books on the market knows that this requires a significant investment in time, a commodity that, like many today, I'm short of. In a single, enjoyable day, Vic presented many of the essential ideas of NLP, emphasising how they can be helpful to musicians. I came away inspired to explore these ideas further and to see how they can be used for my work. Vic is a very effective communicator, which must be proof of the efficacy of the same NLP techniques he covers in this course."

Pete Farrugia, guitarist and teacher

"Since working with Vic Hyland, I have gained an enormous amount of music knowledge. I am now a more confident musician and have played in numerous bands; with the right help and support, I worked through to grade 8 in electric guitar.

Vic's guidance has been instrumental in getting me into teaching, and I have obtained my Music Teaching Diploma in guitar. I am now building a successful career as a teacher in several local schools.

Vic's insights, support and mentoring have been invaluable in developing my guitar playing, confidence and ambition to become an accomplished musician. I could not recommend him more highly as a tutor."

Denise Greenwood, guitarist and teacher

Contents

Acknowledgements

It has been a long journey, a study of over forty years of playing, teaching, creating, listening, and watching. Sometimes the ideas came when I was doing something else, like watching my children and grandchildren grow up, or just while watching nature. I am sure I missed more lessons than I noticed.

There were many occasions when teachings came to me from those around me. I will give a list of names in no order of importance, but they have, all in their way, shaped my thinking and helped form this work.

Firstly my mother, a psychic, started me on this weird path. She was one of the truly remarkable souls one occasionally meets in life, but I was also blessed that she was my mother. My sister Margaret and my brothers Ken and John were role models who looked after me, made me believe in pirates and stories, and planted the seeds of Rock 'n' Roll.

Hannah, Ellie, Rose, and Olivia, I watched, and you instructed me, and you still do.

For those who walked with me for a time – Jessica, Julie, Jane – and Susan, with whom I shared dreams, and Kay and Christine, who unravelled our family tree and added more colour to my father, if ever he needed any more colour!

Laura, Stella, Josh, Carlo, Nick, Mandy, and Stef, for their deep friendship.

The weirdos: Mark, Alenka, Angharad, Vi and Jim, Dave, Marco, Leo, Trish, all of the card slingers from the early days of Coffee and Cards, and its Empresario Elise, and the excellent Dr Rich Edwards, who was dragged into the editing of this book but has added extra depth by his awesomeness.

Without you Mike, Grant, Chris, Tom, Joe, and Sam, BluescampUK would not exist in the world. Thanks also to all the campers and the hundreds of pupils that have been unwitting guineapigs in my mad experiments.

Big thanks to Andrea for the artwork.

Thanks to all the people who have been interviewees on my podcast and have helped in this creative endeavour.

Thanks to John, who helped keep me focused on the book and the charity and helped me in a storm.

Thank you to Barbara and John, two of the most intelligent people I have ever met, who were kind enough not to point out my failings.

Although I've mentioned Mike already, he is worth mentioning again for his friendship and willingness to become a true musician and musical innovator in the world of education.

To Susan, above all, you taught me the complexity of consciousness, through challenging the ways of the world and the journeys we have made. Both the light and the dark, the real and the unreal. I am deeply grateful. May light illuminate your path.

This book will unlock creativity
and change your world.

Foreword

BY KENNY KEMP

The aural pleasure of music enriches our lives infinitely. But few of those who sing, play or perform are instinctively gifted.

To make the most of any given talent, and to learn how to improvise or to interpret another's work, a musician requires the inspiration and direction of a teacher who has experience, empathy and patience.

The best teachers are also those who have experienced the terrific highs and the self-doubting lows of the concert arena. These are the people who can smooth the roughest edges and polish the brilliance.

Vic Hyland is one of those remarkable teachers. He has always thought deeply about what makes a musician tick – and what makes great and memorable music. Through his excellent blog, he has explored the journey of artists and performers in a deeply thoughtful way.

While his forte has been in the rock, blues and popular music genre, he understands where this intersects with more classical forms of music. Vic's encyclopaedic knowledge of musical genres, styles and tonality results in innovation and originality which both sparkles and crackles.

Moreover, Vic has a passion that is infectious. His friendly demeanour and his positivity, coupled with an honesty and laid-back character, has encouraged and fostered scores of talented people for nearly 45 years.

Vic's stories are worth hearing because they reveal a great deal about our combined human experience and how we can evolve, blossom and thrive through the profound nature of sound and music.

Kenny Kemp

Kenny Kemp is an author, journalist, media communicator and one of the UK's most experienced non-fiction writers. He has been engaged as a report writer and media consultant to a number of individuals, businesses and organisations. He has been the preferred ghost-writer to several international business figures.

Kenny is a former daily and Sunday newspaper journalist. He was founding Business Editor of the Sunday Herald and Editor of BQ (Business Quarter) Scotland for five years from 2010 until 2015, and has been a contributor to Scottish Business Insider. He is a former staffer of the Evening Standard in London. He has written comprehensively for a range of titles such as the Herald, Sunday Herald, The Scotsman, and the Sunday Times.

Kenny worked as collaborator with Sir Richard Branson on his best-selling business book, Business Stripped Bare, published in September 2008, and Co-author with Barbara Cassani of Go: An Airline Adventure, WH Smith Business Book of the Year in 2004.

Preface

"Every heart sings a song, incomplete until another heart whispers back. Those who wish to sing always find a song. At the touch of a lover, everyone becomes a poet." - Plato

My path through life and music has taken me to some weird and fascinating places. I almost 'made it' a couple of times, only to have my expectations dashed at the last minute, something which I think is true for many of my fellow musicians. So I learnt to make money by *teaching* music and managed somehow to bring up a family without being away from home too often.

I discovered early on that I had a knack for getting people to play. Perhaps my excitement about my instrument (a guitar) made it possible, because I certainly didn't know what I was doing. I was just able to play, and I was passionate.

I was fortunate to have been born with a keen musical ear, and, like others of my generation, I learnt to play by listening to other musicians' recordings. "Fake it 'til you make it," they say, and I did exactly that, gradually working my way into some good music schools.

I loved to create, write songs, and perform, but I also developed a fascination with what was going on in the creative player's *mind*. From an early age I had been interested in the weird, the illogical, and the paranormal, and this led me to develop an interest in psychological techniques, particularly Neuro-linguistic Programming (NLP). I began to realise that most of the great players and creatives come to music from a left-field perspective, one that is difficult to quantify.

This book attempts to weave these threads into a spider's web, connecting music back to archaic sources of magical potency, from religious music and its folk roots, through to blues, flamenco, Latin, and shamanic traditions.

We will look at the musicians' idea of the groove; that 'soul space' between musicians that informs how the music plays *us*, rather than us playing *it*.

Along the journey I will signpost songwriting techniques that have been used by some of the greatest songwriters of all time, notably originating from a couple of magicians who used similar methods for creating books and artworks ... and for cursing people.

This book is intended to be interactive, so visit www. vichyland.com for resources that back up the essays that form the chapters. I hope you enjoy my indulgence in writing about the things that I am curious and passionate about.

HOW to Use this book

This book explores aspects of creativity in music, both logically and mythically.

The creative arena of thought is a wild, dreamlike terrain that is vast, strange, and dynamic. Consciousness, the 'hard' problem for science, wants to map this landscape logically, but to do so is like grasping smoke. Our predecessors knew this, so they used myth, metaphor, and symbolism to explore and describe its terrain. Through worked examples and thought experiments, and investing (perhaps only temporarily) in the belief that something is true or accurate, we can explore new creative ideas. Let us permit that there are no correct answers and that it is preferable to think of better questions. In this way we can pursue and develop a picture and see where it leads us.

Ideas of magic and psychological tricks are pretty much interchangeable in this book. Those who are comfortable with magic are encouraged to think in those terms, but those who prefer a psychological frame are equally welcome. Many occult magicians, such as Osman Spare, Peter J. Carroll, and Aleister Crowley, co-opted the psychology and science of their time into their work, while the great psychologists, such as Carl Jung, Sigmund Freud, and Wilhelm Reich, incorporated the tropes of magic and mysticism into theirs.

This book is imbued with magic; sometimes in plain sight and sometimes not. For example, we will explore applications of the cut-up method of William S Burroughs and Brian Gysin, as this is an excellent and accessible way to generate ideas that can lead you to exciting places and (hopefully) to revelations about yourself and the world. Techniques drawn from the aforementioned NLP will also be covered. The apparently random nature and sequence of the articles in this book is intended to promote creativity by juxtaposing ideas. Finally, I hope that the imagery will lead you to see reality as malleable, the obstacles facing you as easy to overcome, and open you to becoming comfortable with the fluency of creative thinking.

I have used these techniques and ideas myself over many years to significant effect, and they have helped many others to become creative musicians, actors, and human beings.

Just relax and see where it all takes you; I am sure it will be somewhere more exciting and more abundant in possibility than the previous paradigms you have been taught.

Play with the ideas.

How to use this book – addendum

In the early part of the 20th century, Alistair Crowley produced a book called The Book of Lies. A rather curious title on the face of it, but it speaks to something profound about how we see the world.

Contained within Music, Magic, and NLP are gross simplifications and maybe lies, because whenever we talk about consciousness, we have a problem describing something as elusive. I often refer to the right and left sides of the brain. These terms are problematic now; however, Iain McGilchrist's book *The Master and his Emissary* has revived this idea.

I think it works well as a metaphor to explain the different ways of thinking, one very creative and the other very logical.

In his book *The Brain,* David Eagleman talks of the brain as a city with many things going on simultaneously in different places. A perfect analogy; however, even if sex workers may be busy throughout the city, I postulate that there is also a red light district. I use locations within the brain as an easy way to focus and explain the behaviours for creativity.

We like stories, and a narrative may not be logical or factual, but it is persuasive; it is how we map, and history bears this out. From Christianity to Capitalism, from the Big Bang to Communism, we like a narrative to inform us, give a direction, and create cohesion.

This book of lies contains techniques I have used for many years to help people reach successful outcomes.

Track 1

SERGEANT PAPER'S CARDIOLOGY CLUB

Cut-up

"One must always be careful of books and what is inside them, for words have the power to change us." - Cassandra Clare (Clockwork Angel)

My first use of the cut-up technique was about 35 years ago, when I needed to write songs for a project backed by the record company EMI.

The project started with elements of the band that I played for, fronted by Roger Moore's son Geoffrey. It became evident that we needed to quickly assemble a set to showcase his vocals (which were very good) and highlight other aspects of the band - notably horns, percussion, and guitar.

I was the songwriter for the band and worked with Geoff to put song ideas together. I might have messed about with the cut-up technique before, but this was the first time I used it consistently. It was so effective that I wrote two of the best songs that I'd ever created in a single day, and I was subsequently able to churn out songs of a higher creative aspect than those I had written previously.

Although I was a reasonable songwriter, I usually worked with other people, particularly in the reggae band Bravura, who had a solid songwriting team. We had some pretty standard techniques, mostly of the "let's sit down and write songs ... what ideas have you got?" type of approach. In contrast, the cut-up technique is almost like presenting your unconscious with an open canvas on which to start work.

First let's run through the basic principles (there will be a video available for this in the footnotes or directly from the interactive book) Here we go.

You will need some sources of inspiration, such as colour supplements from newspapers, books on poetry, novels, and anything well-written, perhaps a printout of a blog or some decent online journalism.

Open the book or article at random, and - without hunting - find a phrase. You don't want a complete sentence, just a phrase, then another one, and another, and so on. Keep going until you have filled a couple of sides of A4.

Now go back and see which bits of the text jump out at you. Mark them off and see if they fit together. Your unconscious starts to build a narrative, one which might even say something about you (but that's another story!).

For the moment, just see if you can put the fragments together so that they create a verse. Don't worry about rhyming the words, because they don't need to. If you really want them to rhyme, you can amend them later, but for the time being, just keep the thing flowing.

You might then decide that you want to create a chorus. A chorus needs to be catchy and attract the attention of the people listening. For that, it's probably good to look at headlines for adverts, titles of books, films, chapter headings, etc., because they are designed to attract attention. Repeat the same process with these. You might want things to rhyme this time, or you can achieve a similar effect by repeating something several times (like 'we will rock you', for example). You can develop some really exciting lyrics in this way.

I have some other techniques for folding psychological patterns into songs, but more of that later.

As noted earlier, the cut-up technique was developed by William S. Burroughs and Bryan Gysin, who would incorporate things heard from radio or TV, read from advertising hoardings, or just stuff seen on the street. Burroughs would often go out and record street sounds on an open reel tape recorder and then cut that up and stick it back together again. This, of course, was the beginning of sampling; the guy was a genius.

In the first instance, cut-up gives us a way of quickly assembling lyrics, but it can also be used to create structures for songs, melodies, and chord sequences by doing much the same thing: take some sources that already exist and shuffle them around. Changing the order creates something new.

Thought experiment

Just do it!

If you would like to join us, go to patreon.com/vichyland and find out when the next songwriting or magical songwriting course is running - we go deeper and practice further. The most important thing is to get started, get involved, and do it. Create! Record on your phone, upload the ideas to YouTube or Soundcloud. Work with others.

Spell work

Include in your lyrics, "The words are magic on the page" and "Melodies are rich and beautiful". Include positive intentions for the future.

Sgt Pepper and A Day in the Life

The most iconic album that The Beatles produced was Sgt Pepper. The band's touring life had ended, and the album marked new territory for a pop band: not to play live, but to record their work - in layers in the studio - and rely on radio airplay to promote it.

The influence of Burroughs and Gysin is strongly evident in this album, with the cut-up technique employed in the creation of the album cover as well as the songs.

When you look at the collection of songs, they are seemingly random, from circus-like tracks such as 'Sgt Pepper' and 'For the Benefit of Mr Kite', to the classic Beatles-style pop songs, such as 'Getting Better' and 'With a Little Help from My Friends'. Indian and psychedelic tinged songs include 'Lucy in the Sky with Diamonds' and 'Within You, Without You'. However, the overall collection retains the feel of a concept album.

The song that interests me the most is 'A Day in the Life', as it is pure cut-up. It combines more than one song - one by Lennon and one by McCartney - with some orchestral filler, presumably added by George Martin.

Lennon's opening to his song tells you how it was written, starting as it does with 'I read the news today, oh boy'. The lyrics are excerpts from a newspaper and a film. McCartney's song describes getting ready for work and catching a bus. The piece then finishes with another Burroughs technique - tape recordings being manipulated and sped up to a crescendo for the final chord. As this was an analogue recording, the key changes as the tape increases in speed, so the tape machine itself becomes a musical instrument.

The album cover montage includes Burroughs as one of the heads and The Beatles as circus entertainers in brocaded jackets, with their former selves as the suited and booted 'Fab Four'. also included in the arrangement.

This apparently random collection of songs that hangs together like a well-thought-out masterpiece is classic cut-up, in which random ideas placed on a page create unique poetic ideas. Listen to the album anew and see what you think; you may find there is a lot more to it than you ever noticed before.

I have not even mentioned anything about 'Lucy in the Sky with Diamonds', as I will leave that for you to study.

Thought experiment

Using the ideas sparked by the above songs, create something of your own. It could be observational, like Paul's section of 'A Day in the Life', or it could be a dreamscape like 'Lucy'.

Look at the equipment you use to record your music as musical instruments in their own right. See what you can do creatively with the microphone, computer software, etc.

Have fun. Maybe find a circus poster or create your own.

Spells

Magic uses showmanship, as do shamen. Its inclusion by mystics, gurus, and magicians adds to the power of ritual

- something which is also true of the church. Flipping this around and thinking of the circus troupe makes the magical element more acceptable for many, and maybe this is what makes Sgt Pepper so successful.

Be a showperson.

Mapping your journey

Before we start a journey, we need to know where we are heading. What is our direction? From whence are we starting? At some point our ancestors named the directions North, South, East, and West and directionality became unified and standardised. But there was a time before they were named. Someone made a magical decision to invoke directionality and encoded it into two dimensions as a drawing, in order to have power over it. In other words, they created a map.

Tad James developed his Time Line Therapy™ technique from aspects of NLP and hypnotherapy in the 1980s. He observed that we store memories linearly, with a timeline delineating them. Things get even more interesting when we use dowsing or shamanic journeying techniques on these timelines, though these are not part of the core practice itself.

If making a map is a magical act, then these NLP timelines create an imaginary magical map in time. To discover the directionality of your time, think of something that you did yesterday and consider where it is situated as a memory. Is it behind you to the left? Or is it directly behind you? Think of something you plan to do tonight and then something for tomorrow, then connect those thoughts. Where are they situated relative to the views of the past?

Here is a timeline that you can walk, if you imagine these events on the ground around you.

While you walk your timeline, conjure and experience feelings of success with every landmark achieved, as this adds considerably to the experience and potency of what you're doing. I have classified this as an NLP technique, but really it is a magical evocation of time, space and events.

When you are walking your timeline, visualise and put emotional data into the experience. Do not think about how long it's going to take. Just focus on each step of the journey, with no thought as to why or how it can work. Putting yourself into a state of in-between-ness or non-attachment to the outcome is a very effective technique in creative or magical work. I have no scientific justification for this claim, only my own experience and those of others.

I like to charge these 'happenings' by doubling the intensity of the feelings in my imagination. Think of something you can readily imagine, such as being happy; think of an event that made you happy and focus on that feeling. Has it a physical sensation? Where is that sensation situated? Estimate the 'amount' of it - on a scale of 1 to 10, say - and then double the feeling in your mind. You can reinforce it by saying to yourself, "I feel twice as happy". It really is that simple. If you can go beyond ten in your happiness scale, all well and good!

Thought experiment

The process is to 'walk' the memories and place them on your timeline. Think of a memory to give you an idea of where that lies and then think of some things that you aim to do in the future; this gives you your trajectory.

It is a good idea to keep a journal of this work. I mentioned using dowsing. You could further enhance this experience by leaving gifts for spirits of the timeline or by pulling tarot cards to represent archetypes.

Memory mansions

The Greeks used something similar to a timeline as a memory aid to recall complex details in sequence order: the method of loci. The idea was to imagine a mansion or large building that you can walk around in your imagination. Take a mental journey around the building, placing images and memory triggers on objects and walls to help you organise and remember your thoughts. For example, think of a place that you know well, and as you enter the front door, imagine a notice pinned next to the door handle; this could be the category for which you want to file the memories. Now walk through the door into the hallway, and the first object you see will contain the next memory required in that category.

You can use this memory system on your timeline to deepen your experience, placing events or images that are symbolic and not just visual. Suppose you will be taking a guitar exam in the future, leading to you achieving your degree. Imagine taking the exam and visualising the examiner writing excellent remarks on his report. You could imagine the number of the grade, such as grade 8, as an infinity sign floating in the air and printed certificates floating down like ticker tape with cheering, marching bands playing outside.

Layer in important information, such as musical scale patterns, by drawing them onto the mansion journey, along with other reference data, so that they trigger one another.

It is reasonable to assume that the Greeks learned this memory system from earlier civilisations. Much of our understanding of ancient culture has been slanted towards the Greeks and Romans, as Western culture is classically influenced. According to Victorian and Edwardian scholars, the Greeks and the Romans were the originators of many innovations, but in fact they were not. It is clear now that earlier civilizations, such as the Sumerians and Babylonians, created the number systems that the Greeks adopted. I would further surmise that what we understand as psychology, ascribed to Classical Greece (even the word is Greek), was probably understood by earlier Mesopotamian peoples, who organised society into massive cities with a rich cultural and political life. We must also mention the Chinese, as they were at least the equal of anything from Mesopotamia, and this topic would easily fill another book on the subject.

Cost and memory

Writing something down was very complicated if it had to be embossed into clay or written on papyrus or vellum. Even then, only a few people could write or read, whereas practitioners of memory techniques could commit complex information to memory for free.

We know that Homeric tales, such as the Iliad, were originally memorised and then transmitted orally, and it was a few hundred years before they were written down. We are unsure if Homer existed as a single person; like many famous names from the ancient world, he may never have lived, and even if he did, the tales attributed to him are at least partly mythical. Blind storytellers, however, did exist and required prodigious memories to remember such extensive sagas. We know this is to be true, because even today good storytellers have the capacity for many hundreds of tales in their repertoire.

So the concept of the map and the timeline may be more to do with our cognitive processes regarding how they work than the map itself, just as computers reflect our memory (and this reminds me of the biblical phrase "God made man in his image"). When it comes to humans and God, we create the concept of journeys and time and distance. Maybe these things don't exist as such, but that's how we perceive the world.

A little while ago, it was inconceivable to think of time as being 'unreal', but since the advent of quantum physics, we realise that time isn't as we believe it to be and space isn't what we think it is either. While many people may now understand that time is strange, we haven't quite got around to thinking of distance as being strange yet. Well, apart from walking in a straight line worldwide, where you end up back at the same starting point. However, if we consider Peter J Carroll's theory of the universe as a vorticitating hypersphere, not only are we unknowingly moving in a circle directionally, but perhaps we are moving in a circle of time as well. Therefore, our relationship with time and space is a function of our minds, which brings me to ...

Reverse Time

Think of the self-help books about visualising what you want as if it has already happened. Many of them use the NLP process of working back from the future to your position now, a sort of 'reverse time'.

So the question here is: are they all referring to the same concept? Can they all be wrong? Many authors of such books are involved in sport psychology and business and doing very well, thank you. For example, Anthony Robbins, who coaches sports stars, celebrities, and businesspeople and has a significant following who can attest to the effectiveness of his ideas.

So, for the sceptics: many people have experienced very successful results using these techniques. A case in point is Robbins' work with tennis star Andre Agassi, who had dropped in the seedings to lower than 200 but returned to the top five seeds within a year after being coached by Robbins.

Let us permit ourselves to call this 'magical thinking'. Psychology shies away from this label, and 'NLP' only masks it. However, John Grinder and Richard Bandler published a book on NLP called *The Structure of Magic,* and Garner Thompson's book about the use of language in the medical profession was called *Magic in Practice.* These authors understood that words are magical, and we use them to cast a spell, whether in advertising, politics, or courtship. We are literally spelling them.

Magical thinking is free. Therefore, try it, because if it works, it is fantastic, and if it doesn't work, you haven't lost anything.

Thought experiment

Look at a typical map and see what elements it contains. Now think of your timeline with these map features added to it, like hills and valleys shown as gradients. Think of the landmarks that you can place on your timeline to represent things you need on your journey. Draw it out and make it real, then in an open space, walk it. Walk your timeline. Be creative; place signs you have written out on the path to represent the map you have drawn. Feel the hills and valleys and places that you have created.

Future planning for The Greatest

When I was doing my NLP Master Practitioner training in London many years ago, I talked to a young Sikh about Muhammad Ali, who would tell the story of the fight that was coming up. Muhammad Ali would verbally walk through each round saying when he would knocked his opponent down. Even as a kid, I noticed that the fight would often go precisely the way he said it would. It transpired that Muhammad Ali was future pacing the event by imagining the contest in advance. My friend replied that this was what Sikh Warriors would do before a battle - they would go into the future and fight in the spirit world to ordain the outcome of the conflict.

When Joe Frazier beat Muhammad Ali, his explanation for why he lost was that Joe Frazier had dreamt the fight better on that occasion.

Track 2.

WITH A LITTLE HELP FROM MY FIENDS

How music can change your world

"In Egyptian mythology, the Earth was created by a gesture of a god whose name is not revealed. This gesture was reproduced in the hieroglyphic sign, which is identifiable with that by which the god Hesu created music. The name 'Hesu' translated means 'singer'." - Alfred Sendry

Many people will tell you anecdotally that music is of great benefit to their health and state of well-being. But how about it being a real transformation that can rebuild your health, prolong your life, and change the world you inhabit?

I've been teaching and playing music for over 45 years, and I am very interested in music from an artistic and psychological perspective. I have used NLP alongside music to transform my life and other people's lives.

My search into a deeper aspect of music started many years ago. I was intrigued and nosy about what made successful musicians achieve and create and how they did it. I started the 'Creative' podcast, interviewing artists and getting them to tell their stories to see if I could find any clues. One of the lines of thought that I have focused on is the idea that there are no limits to the possibilities, as is evident in the careers of highly successful people.

I was in a conversation with Ben Thomas, who plays the guitar for Adele. Ben has been her guitarist right from the beginning, meeting her at Brit School. He told me about being invited to her birthday party in her mansion in Beverly Hills and described all the crazy things that happened there - people doing magic tricks, rooms that were like other worlds and other states of mind- and he said that when you meet these high performing and high achieving people, they don't have any limits to what they believe. They believe they can do anything, that anything is possible, and there are no rules.

Hearing this might make us concerned and conflicted, but this probably tells us something about why we are stuck, because we believe there are limits to what we think is possible.

Prince was an excellent example of someone with no limits. Prince's artwork and how he presented himself had blatant magical overtones, such as the use of sigils (remember the logo and the oddly shaped guitar that he played?). He referenced other great musicians, such as Hendrix, Sly Stone, James Brown, and Little Richard, almost becoming them in his performances.

These people achieved unbelievable things with this mindset. We could approach this from a scientific process to test such things out, however you can't test something out with the belief that it will not work. You have to be open-minded, then, if something does work, that is all that should concern you.

I was fortunate enough to do my NLP training with Richard Bandler, Paul McKenna, and Michael Breen, and the former's story about how he arrived with the idea of NLP was particularly fascinating. Richard tells the story that he was an enthusiastic martial artist as a young man, training for many hours a day. However, he was then diagnosed with cancer and was so angry and distraught that he went on a bender and, in his own words, 'woke up in Mexico'. He claimed later that drinking tequila was a great way of destroying cancer cells, but reading deeper into this story, I think he took a pilgrimage to Mexico to meet a shaman following Carlos Castaneda's footsteps in the book The Teachings of Don Juan, as was trendy in the 60s. I am guessing here, but let us assume that Bandler took copious amounts of peyote in the Mexican desert and 'woke up'.

NLP incorporates ideas from shamanic practice, just as Carl Jung's work is indebted to the mystical Christian and Gnostic traditions, though this only became evident after his 'Red Book' was published.

These pioneers decided they needed to 'science up' their work to make it acceptable, which speaks a lot about the situation in which we find ourselves. In our current thought paradigm, if something doesn't fit, it cannot be spoken, and to do so is a form of heresy. Science has become a religion. We have situations where people will not dispute ideas from their teachers until those teachers have died, allowing somebody else to put forward a new hypothesis. This happens in all areas, from science to archaeology, medicine, psychology, and even ESP research.

Thought experiment

Grant Morrison and Alan Moore use psychological/magical ideas in their comic books. Let's look at what music can do.

Let's start with what we *think* music can do. I believe the power of the arts can change the world, so make your belief in music powerful. Change the context and that will change the detail.

At the moment, music and the arts are a commodity. They never used to be. They were powerful and transformed people's consciousness (trance dance in shamanic traditions, for example).

Art is magic, and music is art.

Let us go on a journey.

Magic is Art

"I believe that magic is art and that art, whether that be music, writing, sculpture, or any other form, is magic. Art is, like magic, the science of manipulating symbols, words or images, to achieve changes in consciousness. Indeed, casting a spell is to spell, use words, and change people's consciousness, which is why I believe that an artist or writer is the closest thing in the contemporary world to a shaman." - Alan Moore

In the last 45 years of teaching and playing, I have experienced several extraordinary happenings where simple, ordinary people have become prolific artistic performers. I was unable to spot in advance the ones that would become great musicians, but with the benefit of hindsight, they were the ones who put in the hours, and their ability to play and create crept up on me unannounced.

I have mentioned before that success in the art world is statistically nigh on impossible and therefore having an unrealistic attitude to your ability is actually a great place to start. Another good place to start is with Alan Moore's assertion that we can alter reality by the very things that we do by manipulating symbols, words, sounds, and images to change the minds of the people who listen.

I noticed that many successful songs are influential not because of their poetic quality but due to command-orientated lyrics which demand action on behalf of the listener. Songs such as 'We Will Rock You', 'All Right Now', and even 'Wild Thing' are examples of this technique. Their lyrics have a downward command-oriented inflection and therefore fall into Alan Moore's spellcasting concept.

The very act of subverting reality and your belief in what is possible seems to be an ingredient required from a successful artist. Merely dealing with reality is not enough, and distorting reality is just the beginning. Making people act in a way that corresponds with your distortion of reality is the aim.

We are living in a world where facts and truth are being trumped, literally and metaphorically, by the emotional aspects of language like never before, and we particularly see this in politics. We also see it constantly in the media. It is abundantly clear that emotional soundbites are far more effective than reasoned arguments and are longer-lasting. Evoking the spirit of Englishness or Americanness is powerful, but we must be very careful to look after that evocation because even a cuddly cat, if mistreated, has a very dark side to it, and so does Englishness.

Being more positive about Alan Moore's quotation means that we can do incredible things if we picture them and then formulate sounds that bring that vision to life. Look at the successful music of bands such as Queen. Think of any of their famous songs, which genuinely seem to have a life of their own, and when you hear the music, you see Freddie Mercury. Magical!

Thought experiment

Do what it takes to get you into a receptive (magical) state of mind; for example, by reading an incantation or watching or reading some Alan Moore, Grant Morrison, Ursula Le Guin, or J.K. Rowling. I've even seen NLP techniques evoking Mickey Mouse, Kermit, and Ganesha, so whatever is your jam.

Then, in this state, create some art. Make, write, paint … as you focus on your intention, forget about the logic and lose yourself in the art.

See what happens over time, commune with your works of art, feed them by leaving water, whisky, or chocolate offerings, or whatever feels right for you.

The song already lives

Keith Richards once said in an interview that songs are out there, all around you, and all you need to do is to reach out and grab one. I like this idea and the possibility that we do not have thoughts, but thoughts have us.

How else to explain the ideologies that surface and then infect people, from the political thoughts and theories we become obsessed with to the memes that abound on the internet.

I often wonder what happened to the flashers and the streakers who literally exposed themselves in the 1970s. Did they all go away? What possessed people? Was this some form of the trickster, perhaps? Did the trickster become something else in the 1980s, but clothed this time?

Turn things around: thoughts having us, instead of us having thoughts. Helping thoughts manifest and ideas gain some form of agency or spirit is a powerful technique, as it breaks the creative sensor and allows us to write imaginatively. I like the NLP proposal that 'it doesn't matter if it's not real, does it work?' Considering thoughts as having some agency enables us to 'invoke' ideas and removes the personal creative burden to create something from nothing.

We need to open our minds for new ideas to enter, like the muses of old, to inspire and infect us. We need to be irrational, willing to take thoughts and turn them around; black needs to be white, white needs to be black, the unreal needs to be the real, and the actual needs to be imaginary.

If you need a character to speak to you for a book or a song, invite them into the room, sit on an empty chair, and have a conversation.

The scientific method is excellent, but it is a tool. Scientism is like believing in an electric drill's redemptive quality. Belief belongs to the world of the unconscious, and that is where it is most effective.

Maybe we can change our lives by writing songs. Life mimicking art is an idea that has concerned people before, and there are strange examples of musicians and artists whose lives started to follow the work they had produced. This has happened to me on many occasions, taking me from 'that is funny', to 'that is odd', to 'that is crazy' to 'I need to create songs that speak of better outcomes'.

The old bluesmen knew that songs had the power to change things. The old blues songs were active, in the sense of things being able to change. In other words, 'If my baby don't love me no more, I know her sister will'.

Thought experiment

Invite the song in and write it as a dictation. You are part of the alchemy of the song, so direct its manifestation.

Allow the song to move positively through you while you add to it, steering it to your better future.

LSD WITH GEMS

The world is made of words

"The world is made of words, and if you know the words that make the world, you can create whatever you wish." - Terence McKenna

In the beginning was the word. It is certainly true that once we have a name for something, we have some way of controlling it. Like with music: if we know what key it is in, what the chords are, how the rhythm is constructed, and we have labelled these with words, we then have a way of manipulating this information and transferring the ideas to something else.

We need to give a voice and name to what we want, but we are too frequently encouraged to contemplate what we do not want in our lives, such as illnesses, depression, lack of money ... all because someone is making money out of our fear.

Think about the words that you use within your work and in your day-to-day life. Be aware of the power of the words being used on you. This is not a new thing. It has been done for millennia through state religion – being told from the pulpit what to believe and how to be. Now it is achieved through the media, and I am sure that when we look back, we will see how ridiculous our current times are, in the same way that we now recognise that 1940s and 50s Pathé newsreels were condescending, speaking to the naïve in patronising tones.

Speak in a commanding way, using words that create the desired outcomes. We need to see, hear, and recognise the words used to control our lives and take back control from the media and society in general.

It is time to wake up now and build a new life with new words. Consider why songs are powerful. Listen to the following songs in the days to come: 'We will Rock You', 'Wild Thing', 'Riders On The Storm', 'All Right Now', 'Moondance', and 'The Boys Are Back in Town'.

Add to this list. The above are command-driven lyrics telling you something. Not asking you, telling you, with authority.

So go and change things.

Thought experiment

Write some commanding phrases, such as, 'they love me here', 'be good to me always', 'my love shines in the world, now.' Print these out and stick them on your wall or get a pen for writing on glass and write them on your bathroom mirror at home, so you read the message every time you look into it.

Stealing fire from the gods

Myths are full of stories of the trickster stealing the fire from the Gods. Much of the creative process is about taking something that is not yours and appropriating it for yourself.

There is much handwringing about appropriating from other traditions, but music has always done this, and so have language and magic. It is as if we are stealing fire from the gods, taking something that wasn't meant for us, but there is no going back once we have stolen it.

There is something of the trickster in every artist and musician that is worth their salt, a way of subverting what is the norm, applying a skill from another discipline and making something new or redesigned. It always comes with its own significant personal risk to the artist. The great thieves are the greatest beneficiaries: Bowie, Hendrix, Osman Spare, and Philip K. Dick are good examples.

Instead of just copying something else or learning something by rote, it's more a case of stealing it and then hot wiring it, reworking it, and passing it off like stolen goods.

I'll give you a couple of examples here. Jimi Hendrix's 'Voodoo Chile' riff is stolen from John Lee Hooker or Muddy Waters, but whenever you hear it, you think of Jimi.

Another example is Hendrix's seven sharp nine chord, which is in most of his songs, plucked straight out of jazz and put into rock. Different musicians have reused his favourite guitar chord after Hendrix used it. An example is Free's 'Mr Big' and Stevie Ray Vaughan's 'Scuttle Buttin'.

Thought experiment

Steal an idea or a technique and work on it to make it yours as if you are passing off stolen goods as your own.

Enjoy the feeling of transgression - it is a powerful feeling that you can harness as Taboo Breaking. Add this to your artistic pallet.

Prepare yourself for the gods to come after you, and appease them with offers of songs, food, and libations.

Music is a game

Music is a game best played with others, but it's also ok to play it alone, as long as it makes you happy. If you teach music, happiness is essential to your success.

If music is your business, make it a game, and you can get the love back into it if it has become a chore.

Some of the membership forums about music teaching that I am involved in have horror stories about the pupil who is a walking disaster or the pushy parent wanting their kid to do grade 10 or whatever. My solution is to view it as a game and have a little bit of fun, bringing more success for you and the pupils.

For instance, if someone turns up who has not done any practice - which, let's face it is incredibly common - think about the game you are playing. They turn up and pay you to spend time playing the guitar. So, help them practice, take their money, tell them to have an extra lesson, work towards a concert, and get focused. Organise the gig to play to their friends, a video for the song they created for YouTube, or do an exam.

The pushy parent game is 'Yes, they can do those grades, but for them to have a good chance of passing, they will need to do twice the number of lessons'. Do not concern yourself with the pupil's psychological well-being because if they are under pressure with your guitar lessons, they will be under more significant pressure elsewhere. Your guitar lessons are a drop in the ocean, and what they can learn in self-confidence from music will enable them to grow.

With disorganised schools and colleges, play the trickster game of 'can we do some catching up lessons?'

in which pupils share lessons, and you can catch up on the lesson numbers that way. I also call this the 'statistics game', and governments do it all the time. You are doing this because the pupils have examinations or concerts coming up and you need to get the time in to cover for errors made by the school (which also happens to make you look outstanding in everyone's eyes).

Pupil turns up without music? Then we will do improvisation today. Pupil turns up without their instrument? Then they can use yours and do some songwriting or history of music, etc. It is easier to deal with problems if you do not see them as problems but as opportunities.

Make music a game that the pupils are a part of. Get them to create the rules for this game, such as 'what will they practice this week?' If they complete that, 'what are they going to treat themselves to?'

When working with others, make the game about getting the job done. For instance, the rehearsal could finish early if you get all of the songs completed. I would always conduct band practices this way. We would construct a list that we needed to complete and then work through the list as quickly as possible. When it is completed, you go home.

If you get some miserable so-and-so who doesn't want to play the game, create the game for yourself. One of you might as well have some fun.

What happens when a song casts a spell?

"Are you going to Scarborough Fair?
Parsley Sage Rosemary and Thyme
Remember me to one who lives there
She once was a true love of mine." – 'Scarborough Fair'

What if a song changes reality? I believe that such songs exist. 'All You Need is Love' by the Beatles may not be the sole cause of the 'Summer of Love' but I'm sure it increased its potency as it rode the crest of that wave in 1967.

'Heroes' by David Bowie, released in 1977, included references to the Berlin Wall and its ultimate failure, and Bowie's Berlin concert led to the sudden taking down of the wall in 1989. Ripples in the pool caused by art? Who can say?

I am particularly interested in the songs written by people that hint at their ultimate demise. For instance, 'Son of a Gun' by Kurt Cobain and 'Happiness is a Warm Gun' by John Lennon are notable examples.

Tim Buckley's 'Song to the Siren' foretells his son's death by drowning many years later. And it gets weirder than that: Elizabeth Fraser of the Cocteau Twins covered the song and later recorded it with Tim's son Jeff Buckley, and the two became lovers. Jeff became the unnamed character in the song and later drowned in the Mississippi in a freak accident.

What about the song that takes us back in time through our memories or makes us cry or laugh? We all have examples of that, I am sure. What is this mysterious power that music has?

In folk music, there are lots of examples of songs that have some magical intent. Some songs seem to be curses, while others describe impossible tasks, popular amongst the cunning folk as they went about their business. A piece such as Scarborough Fair has several impossible tasks asked of an ex-lover, such as making a shirt with no seams and no needlework and washing it in a dry well. It also includes a list of protective herbs, such as sage, rosemary, and thyme, which were believed to be particularly useful against witchcraft. Does this mean that the ex-lover in question was a witch?

Also within British folk music were references to magical trees and birds and enchanted people who met with the Faery folk. In some traditions, the good folk gifted them a skill such as playing music, while other tales warned that it might not go well dealing with the realm of the Faery.

A rich tradition of magical practice within the blues is most evident in Muddy Waters' and Robert Johnson's songs. Many of Muddy Waters' songs, viewed through the lens of NLP or magical thinking, look like some form of hypnotic suggestion, such as 'I've got my mojo working (but it sure don't work on you)'. Take out the negative and there you have a magical love spell cast on anyone who Muddy Waters fancies in the audience.

So I thought it was about time to explore songwriting possibilities using phrases that intend an outcome. We can do this in many ways, such as:

All you need is love,
All you need is love,
All you need is love, love,
Love is all you need.

I think this last line is particularly clever in that it is a reworking of the first line, and then, of course, the end of the song is a mantra; 'Love is all you need'.

In the outro, the song references other songs that include love, such as 'She Loves You'.

Recall a memory with some emotional resonance for you. Just remembering that thought will bring the original emotional resonance. Consider the word 'remembering' - it tells you what is happening. You literally put back together that thought in all its parts.

Now that we have realised what a piece of art can do, let us be aware of our responsibility. No more songs to take you to the dark places in yourself unless you specifically want to experience that. Let us use the pieces we create to take us, and others, to better places.

One more thing. Writing a song that can make your life better costs nothing (though recording it in a studio might). Making it happen in the world also costs nothing: record it on your phone, write the lyrics out, and put them on the wall. The effects can be amazing! Believe me, I have been teaching this to people for years, and the results are mind-blowing. So, all you need is … to start spelling it out.

Make a song that changes your life.

CONSTANT IMPROVEMENT

Magic has been drained out of history by the historians

"Magic has been drained out of history by the historians." - Gordon White

A fundamental omission in re-telling the past - not just in our own history but also how we understand ourselves - is the role of magic. It is difficult for us to reconnect with our predecessors' fundamental belief in magic; it infused everything they did. By extension, music and art were a magical connection with the other world.

It is impossible to understand why or how people thought without reinserting that fundamental belief in magic and the supernatural back into history. We also have to respect those people and remove ourselves from our colonial Western mindset and the arrogance that we have the answers, because we do not. With a little bit of humility, we can see that our ancestors' beliefs and their use of magical rituals and spiritual practices gave rise to incredible innovations in art and technology. For us, our focus will be what this type of thinking did in relation to music.

Music and art invoked and evoked altered states of consciousness, and our ancestors knew that. Their definitions of how these things happened would differ from ours - we will explain them using psychological terminology - but anybody who is a student of Carl Jung will understand that psychology is only a cipher for magical thinking, as evidenced by *The Red Book.*

I would say that today music is disconnected from this otherness. It has little or no inner energy, which is why root styles of music frequently come back into the popular music arena and re-energise music, disguised as rock and roll, punk, reggae, or grunge, and something innately visceral and otherworldly.

One thing that one could say about modern pop music is there is very little that is magical about it. Often it is so computerised and quantised that any energy essence has been removed and replaced with something sterile. However, if the computer remains the servant and not the master, the DJ producer's heart can be 'bound' into the songs. Dance is an excellent example of this; I think the deciding point here is, were any risks taken? Producing a song by Rihanna or Katy Perry may be more a case of not getting it wrong than getting it right because of the big budgets involved.

We find it very difficult to think in a mediaeval way because progressivism has indoctrinated us to believe that much of what they believed was nonsense, but clearly their ideas were practical and worked for them. If, however, you ask yourself why ritualistic behaviour and magic systems seem to be highly conserved, remaining largely unchanged for two millennia, why would we keep doing something that does not work? The logical answer to that question is that it did. It is only we that have rid ourselves of the magical tools from the toolbox.

For an example of magic being inherent in nearly

everything in post-enlightenment times, I shall return to the words of Scarborough Fair. I have never seen anything mentioned about the witchcraft element in this song. It is only because of my interest in history, particularly 'folk' history, that I became aware of the song's implications.

Several ancient hymns display magical thinking. The most obvious are the wassailing songs and the Holly and the Ivy, which symbolises Christian mysticism. One rather bawdy version of this pre-dates the version collected by Cecil Sharp and mixes the profane with the sacred.

I suggest that by looking back at styles that may influence us musically and getting to the root of what drives it, we can reconnect with what the music is about and derive something from it to reanimate the music that we play.

Thought experiment

You do not have to believe in magic and the supernatural, only suspend your disbelief to unlock the unconscious. I would suggest listening to musical styles such as Blues or Flamenco or the English folk music tradition and see what sort of weirdness you can find in there: mojos, dances of the spider (the tarantella), impossible tasks asked of ex-lovers, etc. Pull on that thread a little and see where it takes you.

Go back to old history books and reread them, and this time put the magic back in. See what effect this has on your understanding of something like the Black Death and people's belief in the tenets of Christianity, as there was a documented drift away from the church at this time.

Put yourselves into the shoes of the people and bring back the supernatural.

Then maybe head off to the crossroads to talk to Old Nick.

The creatures called Chords

"We learn that chords are living things." - Jimmy Webb

Any good songwriter will tell you that chords have a natural gravity to them. Some will say that they seem to hold a dialogue with you through the music. They inform you as to what is coming next, and they also tell you what is not coming next. When we play a chord that is incorrect in the sequence, it screams at us. All music does this - melodies, voicings of chords, and harmonies - if they are wrong. I have found it easy to understand this in music by adopting a pseudo-animist perspective, believing that the song lives.

Consider the great songs' impacts. Some have spanned generations; others burn brightly for a short period and then disappear. Often there is no logical reason why a piece should last for so long, but music and the arts are not subject to intellectual reasoning, and the reality of art and music is in the imaginal.

It is evident to many thinkers that this subliminal or imaginal world is powerful and 'real'. Carl Jung believed that if you don't listen to what your unconscious has to say to you, it will become manifest in the material world as a problem; as an illness or a psychological disturbance.

There are fascinating comparisons between Jungian 'active imagination' exercises and processes that artists go through to create a piece of work, even being 'taken over' by the song in order for it to find its way into the world.

This way of thinking is sadly absent from the education system that teaches such things as creative writing. Still, if songs have real agency and may have a way of changing things, this is a tremendously powerful influence and something that we should bear in mind. Even if you don't believe in the efficacy of what I am saying, even the ability to write better songs with this way of thinking should be reason enough to adopt some of those ideas.

Thought experiment

Speak to the chords and allow songs to rise unhindered from any intellectual strictures. For those interested in Jungian active imagination exercises, I recommend episode 13 of the 'This Jungian Life' podcast[1.]

Make even the most straightforward chord sequence come to life by acknowledging the chords as sentient beings that are working for you in the song. Listen to the chord sequence and, in an unfocused way, allow the sounds to arise; they could be melodies or just sounds.

Listen to the ideas they have. What have they got to tell you? What can you learn from them? Don't judge them. And - as with all things - the more you do it, the better you will become.

What's your problem?

"If the problem is big enough and the solution good enough, then you have the potential for starting a successful business."
- Brett Slazenger

Brett set up the very successful Drum Café from this entrepreneurial observation. However, artistic people generally start from a different place.

In my lectures to musicians at conferences, I note that we usually start from the perspective of a hobby and

---

1   https://thisjungianlife.com/ep13/

then try to turn it into a business or career. As a result, we often end up making the decisions of a hobbyist and not an entrepreneur. I think it is essential for us to change our mindset if we aim to make money from music. Think like an entrepreneur and see opportunities that are solutions rather than problems. Unemotional entrepreneurial thinking based on an independent state of mind that is unlike the hobbyist's approach. We buy something because it makes money, either directly or indirectly; we do not buy it because we want it.

It is challenging for artists to try to be unemotional or achieve something that solves a problem without creative thinking, but the clues are out there. Although we are selling to an emotion, we should not be emotional.

A lot of my teaching work caters for younger people (from eight years of age up to late teens), and of course they are not paying for the lessons themselves - it's normally their parents or grandparents.

Many parents see music as an essential aspect of life, and it may be because they were unable to make music or because they had a good experience in relation to music that they want to pass on to their children. Plus, of course, it gets them away from the computer screen and games console for a bit.

This brings me back to Bret Slazenger's business. The problem he addressed was getting people in big conferences to look away from their laptop and smartphone screens and to be present in the room. And what better way to do this than to drum with several thousand other people for thirty minutes to an hour?

Brett saw the problem that he was solving to be 'screen time'. This could well be the same problem that you will be solving for parents who wish their children to have music lessons. There is no quick fix to a problem like this, because, if there were, everybody would be doing it. You have to keep your eyes open, observe what is problematic, and be open to creative solutions.

When I started playing music, the thing that drove me was a sense of identity, which set me apart from other kids. I looked at people who played the guitar and thought they were cool, and I wanted to be like that. I had already realised I was artistic, and a good chess player, but I did not feel that I was good enough at either. However, I was confident that there might be an opportunity for me to play contemporary rock or blues guitar regardless, and I soon realised that others wanted to learn too and that I could help solve their problem.

Music's psychological aspect is a significant point to consider because it opens an entirely different set of possibilities.

For people with mental conditions and learning difficulties, music can be very beneficial. It also enables people to look at and embrace the world through music, which is an important consideration.

So what is your problem?

A journey

Back into what we would call prehistory, in a building on the bank of the Nile sits a group of acolytes and several of what we might call shamanic priests.

Through the darkness and the thick clouds of aromatic incense, figures were moving. The sacred drink they imbibed profoundly influenced the initiates as the master sang - the dreams at first distant shimmering and resonating to the music.

Geb was a young man, possibly 15 in our years, now at the culmination of years of training. Although not the end of his learning journey, this was a meaningful ceremony that marked a fundamental transition.

The dreams came on … at first, his eyes were full of sleep, the familiar sense of nausea from the brew that he had drunk, never pleasant, was churning his insides, making his head spin.

The shaman's melodic enchantments were now beginning to weave their way in his mind. Each inflection of the song became a picture of strange black and white shapes combining and twisting like a serpent.

Then came the butterflies, and odd lines and shapes flitted across his mind. The butterflies, beautiful and peculiar, came up close and stared directly into his eyes. It seemed as if the insect had sucked him in - he was looking through the eyes of the insect at a world of pin-pick images, and the music rhythmed with the beat of his wings.

As the feeling subsided, he sat wrapped in his thoughts. He looked up and could see silhouettes. Some he recognised, others seemed like giants; he shut his eyes and fell deeper into his reverie.

There she was, a towering figure dressed in beautiful ornate robes which rippled and glistened. There was a heady aroma of sandalwood and sensual spices. She took Geb's hand and spoke sweetly, "I have always been here," she said. "I am your mother."

And with that, he became immersed in her sea, floating, waiting ... how beautiful it was.

He watched, his toes and fingers tingling, as a feeling of urgency started - seemingly from the outside but coupled with a sense from within.

There was a distant cry, and he felt drawn to the tributary, twisting down as he went. Out he came to the cries of the mother, mixed with the song of the priest.

The goddess picked him up, kissed and held him to her breast.

As he suckled, the stars came to look. He saw their twinkling lights surrounding him, and he looked out with eyes open. The room became stardust as he lay like a colossus in the heavens. "Oh, Isis," he thought, "Oh blessed Isis."

In a room, alone by a fire, watching the flames dancing and casting shadows, there in the roof, he could see a cocoon hanging. As he watched, he marvelled at the butterfly in swaddling clothes, transforming from caterpillar to angel, just hanging there suspended between the worlds. In a state of death, it felt familiar.

Moving up and up and into the chrysalis, he shook his head and opened his eyes. The priest was looking directly at him as he sang and cast his incantations into the air.

The wise old man was standing next to him. Geb caught his attention; he was never sure of this crazy character who never spoke much, and when he did it was only ever a series of riddles. Now, this wizened little man seemed to have a majesty that he had not noticed before.

The wise man stared at him. The journeyer was drawn deeper into his eyes, a guttural drawl spinning into his consciousness as he was sucked in. Flying with a bird, an eagle of the desert, unknowable, over the river Nile, glistening below. The goddess-mother said, "These are your tears ... these are the tears of all who live and die and live."

After some time, he found himself in an empty room. He must have slept. The fire had burnt down, and he could see the chrysalis hanging empty, but there was the emergent moth, a strange little creature with eyes on its wings and fern-like antenna. It fluttered down and landed on his shoulder as he exhaled, feeling deeply relaxed.

"Come with me," he heard the moth say. He felt himself lift and fly, not sure whether he was the moth or whether he was on its back.

It flew through the darkness, drawn to the light. The world seemed so different through the eyes of the moth as it fluttered around in its chaotic flight.

The moth is drawn towards the fire; the wild man grabs it and stuffs it into his mouth.

The acolyte was again cast into the abyss. There were battles, strange tunnels, talking trees, and moments sitting in the desert with visits from demons and angels, creatures in animal form, and some with no shape. Stories took on deeper meanings, and everything seemed so funny. Like the cat, who now visited him and head-butted for attention, licking his hands, wanting to be stroked.

The cat looked at him, interested; he felt his nose twitch and his hands change into little paws. He had become a tiny mouse.

The cat eyed him with a strange compulsion, and there was nothing he could do - with a bite to his neck, he lay paralysed. She toyed with him for a while, then, with one gulp, everything went black.

He became aware of a distant singing, echoing deeply. Was it coming from the cat's head? A light appeared in the darkness, coming towards him. The mad priest appeared out of the dark, then, looking at the tiny rodent, smiled. Then, with a touch of his hand, there was light.

He found himself standing by the river; the sun blazed down, and he could hear the songs echoing across the Nile.

He noticed a snake from a distance; it climbed onto a branch to get a better look. "Eat this," said the snake, motioning to a date hanging from the tree. The mad priest looked on.

Geb reached out and pulled the fruit from the branch. As he bit into it, he suddenly knew all manner of things, and the teachings took on a more profound resonance, as if all things had layers of meaning. He marvelled at his thoughts, and he became aware of observing them, detached and with their spirit.

The serpent and its scales, beating heart, and flicking tongue were his; looking through the snake's eyes, he felt his body twist and coil as he became it. His head fanned out, cobra-like, as the serpent energy moved up his spine, and he as the serpent appeared out of his forehead.

The soul of the creator showed itself as the viper. It travels up the tree of life, the tree of knowledge, the tree of the world.

Geb fell into a deep sleep as the mad priest sang incantations to the spirit of the plant.

Commune with nature

Sit under a tree

Laura sat under a tree. It was her favourite, one that she had built a relationship with over the years. She sat with her back against the trunk, took several deep breaths, and relaxed into the feeling.

Each breath took her down, the relaxation more intense with every breath, and her thoughts merged with the tree as she felt it swallow her in its embrace. Deep into its sap she went, a green woman sinking silently into the verdant roots.

At its base there was a lake. Laura slipped into its waters and heard a voice softly singing. She sang the melody and became one with the sound, imagining herself leaping like a salmon. She heard a voice say, "Jumping upstream is what we do." And as she sang, more words came and more melody, until, gradually,- the song arrived. The tree started to suck her up, a new shoot slowly emerging into her body.

Laura took some more deep breaths and said her thanks as she sat with her shoulders against the tree. Removing a notepad from her jacket, she wrote the words down and sang the melody into her phone. Placing some oats around the tree as an offering, she kissed its bark and left for home as a butterfly circled in the air above her.

A walk in nature

Joe was walking in the early morning light through a woodland. He often took this walk, and focusing on his breathing and physical movements, he could reduce the number of ideas and thoughts circulating in his mind.

He imagined the path he was walking inside himself, each step moving further into his unconscious. He became aware of a man slightly smaller than himself leaning against a tree just in front of him, waiting.

Joe stopped, and the man nodded and stood up straight and walked to join him on the path. "I was wondering when you would come," the man breathed. "I wanted to talk about your father."' He continued, "He was distraught but what he did was wrong." Joe felt a tingling of rage or sorrow at this. Unsure which, he breathed deeply.

"Your song needs to change. Make it sweet and change your mind."

Joe's eyes started to tear up, and as the man started to sing, Joe began to weep. Grabbing his notebook and pen, he began to write. The ideas flowed like his tears, cathartic. The dream faded, but the feeling of being watched remained.

Joe said thanks, clapped his hands, and spun around to cast the feelings out. A small yellow butterfly danced in the sunlight above him.

By a river

The river was high, and as Michael reached the bridge, the sun began to shine. He sat by the riverbank and rested on his rucksack, watching the water glistening as it passed.

You cannot enter the same river twice, he thought. This is true of everything; maybe each day we are different people with different thoughts, not to mention the many different cells. Looking back in time to early versions of ourselves, they are sometimes unrecognisable to us.

Permaculture recognises that the spaces in-between, such as the edges of forests, the countryside, towns, land,

and sea are often the most diverse ecologically. Michael pondered this and thought that this might also be true of the unseen world. He stared at the underside of the bridge as a space in-between.

Liminal spaces may have a higher population density of the beings of the spirit world. He got so many ideas in places like this. Bridges, the feet of hills, and the tops of mountains were among his favourites.

Michael was well on his way to finishing his book. He was crafting the novel as a flow of consciousness. He was unaware of what he was jotting most of the time, as if it was some form of automatic writing. He would take these ideas back and craft them, cutting out the deadwood to making the lines more robust and fluent.

He watched as a chalk blue butterfly fluttered before him in the sunlight. A creation that understands metamorphosis, from a caterpillar cared for by ants to the beautiful butterfly that depends on humans and sheep for its existence.

By the sea

Sophie walked across the beach towards the rocks on the far side, feeling the breeze and smelling the sea air. She could almost hear the siren song of the mermaids as she walked.

Her footsteps marked the sand, telling the sea who she was: her weight, her gender, her way of walking. By the time she had reached the far rocks, she had told the sea a great deal, and the sand began to tell its story, of pirates and wreckers and the creatures that live between the land and the deep ocean.

The seventh wave gave its name to Sophie's song, and as she settled on the rocks in the sun, a butterfly landed on the rock next to her. This seemed such a good omen. Delicate and beautiful, it sunned itself before setting off.

Sophie could now see a pirate ship and its crew appearing in the distance, being called to the rocks by the siren where she sat.

For Sophie, the imaginary world was always close, always speaking to her of a richer experience than the life she had left behind before becoming an artist.

Blues at the crossroads

Johnson, disoriented, walked towards the crossroads. There was the usual chirping of crickets, but there was an unusual chill in the air considering how warm it was.

The moon hung in the sky, casting silver shadows on the crossroads ahead. Something was different about this place; he had been here before; however, it was more dreamlike this time. The very fact that he was out, alone in the darkness, and had no idea what was out there waiting for him. He could see the big oak tree; his mind raced.

He was in a very vulnerable place, but it wasn't that kind of fear that he felt. It was more of a tingling on the back of the neck feeling, of someone watching, a creeping uncertainty. There was a smell of something different. A chill that was somehow otherworldly. Johnson had wandered into a dream; he was half expecting to see some long-lost lost aunt just sitting there, waiting on the fence for him. He sat, having arrived in good time, put his whiskey bottle to one side, along with the glasses, and waited.

He waited for what seemed to be a long time and started to feel bored. The fear of being set upon had left him, and he undid the straps of the case, took his guitar out, and started playing and singing quietly.

Johnson guessed that midnight had long gone, and if there were anything strange about this character, he would've turned up at midnight, like in the old stories. He was beginning to lose faith in this man turning up at all, and the situation seemed more and more ridiculous as time went on.

But he just sat and played and sang. He heard a voice which appeared to be coming from the other side of the crossroads, but he was not sure … then, there he was, a man dressed in black, very straight, carrying a walking stick.

"You play well, boy."

"Thank you, sir. Mr Brown told me to meet you, sir, Mr Willie Brown. He said that you would be able to fix my guitar for me."

The man walked across the road and fixed him with a stare and leaned upon his stick; Johnson looked up.

"Are you the man I'm supposed to be meeting?"

"That I am," he said.

"Mr Brown said nothing about you. He didn't tell me your name, just told me to meet you here and to bring some whiskey."

The man in black lifted his hand as if to interrupt the conversation.

"Let me see your guitar." Johnson handed the guitar to him.

He held it, as if to weigh it. He looked down the neck, looked at the machine heads, looked inside the box, then turned a few pegs as if to tune it and strummed the open strings.

He handed it back to Johnson.

"Play it now, boy. Play it."

Johnson started to play, and it was like a new guitar. The action was better but it was more than that; his fingers danced over the guitar in ways he had never known before.

It played so easily it was like it was playing itself. Ideas were coming out of Johnson's fingers, not out of his head - it was enchanting, and he played, and he played.

"What the hell is going on?" Johnson thought, but it felt so good, terrific in fact, like all the blocks that he'd had in the past had just disappeared. He didn't sound like anybody else anymore, he just sounded like ... wow.

"Do you like that?" said the man in black.

"Yes, I like that a lot," Johnson said. "But I don't understand."

"It just needed a little adjustment; a little, let's say ... transformation," said the dark figure. "But now it will play for you like it never did before.

"All instruments, when they are in the hands of someone they trust, will play for them. They have a soul, and sometimes we need to speak to the soul of that instrument to gain its trust. It will begin to dance; it will play through you, like some form of magic, a trick cast by someone who knows."

Johnson was amazed at what was going on with his guitar, his fingers, and his voice. He reached for the whiskey and poured two drinks, and they toasted.

The man looked at Johnson and said, "Now, boy, go and play. You have a gift; use it."

"Thank you, sir," said Johnson, "but how do I pay?"

"Just by going and playing. Lots of doors will open for you. People will love you, but one thing, I warn you …" Johnson looked at him. "Do not," he paused, "do not take any of my women."

Johnson was puzzled at this. "OK," he said, "I'll remember that."

Nodding, the dark figure shook Johnson's hand and said, "Then we have a deal."

The man in black took the whiskey and crossed over to the other side, disappearing into the shadows.

The dark figure had transformed Robert Johnson's life, and he became the greatest bluesman of his time, recording a classic album that influenced the future of music. People say that Johnson's life was mysterious and that even his death was mysterious, murdered by a jealous husband. Johnson had built a reputation as a womaniser, and maybe one of those women may have belonged to the man he met at the crossroads.

FIXING THE WHOLE

Religious Music

"The only proof he needed for the existence of God was music."
- Kurt Vonnegut

The story of Western classical music is the story of religious music. Religious church music is the reason for written music, describing harmony and chords and counterpoint. Some of the greatest - if not the most outstanding - musicians spent much of their time creating sacred music.

Chordal harmony is considerably newer, being only a few hundred years old. It developed in the monasteries, where monks, who had spent a few hundred years singing single-line melodies, had started to experiment singing in two-part harmony, which later developed into something that we would recognise as chordal harmony. I am interested in how and why this innovation happened in the West, whereas it did not in the East.

As far as I can tell, Western monks were 'singing' the sacred texts in larger communities and buildings, whereas in the East, chanting and singing in the more open communities meant that they were more often smaller in number.

Eastern philosophy emphasises impermanence, so their musical traditions are more transient and 'in the moment'.

In contrast, the Western perspective has more of a feel of the word of God being sacred and is therefore more fixed and less open to interpretation, which I believe has given rise to the need for holy hymns to be 'perfected'.

Over the years, Christianity gave rise to musical harmony, with laws to prevent the use of certain intervals that were deemed heretical, moving it away from the Arabic-sounding harmonic minor scale and the augmented second interval. These were very common in Eastern music and Flamenco but were not deemed appropriate for Christian worship.

Accordingly, Western religious music needed to be written down and not made up as an improvisation, unless stringent guidelines were followed. Hence, we get the development of musical theory, qualified musicians, and the drive for musical literacy, and this gives rise to the modern concept of the adept musician being a reader of music.

However, the critical point is that music is a spiritual force, and this was realised by the church, and the text and the notes therefore required supervision. Musicians were passionate about the religious music they created; if you listen to Bach's spiritual music, it is difficult not to be swept away by its power.

Years ago, I heard a story that Bach would phrase or place the name of Jesus in the score so that the first syllable would be on a sharp and the second note for the second syllable would rise to the note above; therefore, Jesus would ascend from the cross.

In trying to validate this story, I spoke to several people who are involved in performing Bach's music. The response I received on each occasion was, "I did not know about this, but it does not surprise me!" Then they would proceed to tell me something else that was incredible about his work.

Bach's deep interest in numerology, reflected in his use of the number three to signify the Trinity, and key words were situated carefully within the music, such as placing the word 'tomb' on a low note, whilst 'heaven' is placed on a high note.

Pieces of music dedicated to the Trinity emphasised threes; for example, the work would consist of three sections, the music might be in a key with three flats (such as E flat major), etc. Other mystical numerological associations were also incorporated, such as seven lots of three (therefore 21) parts or sections.

Within German musical rhetoric, the key of D minor represents death. An example is Schubert's composition 'Death and the Maiden', whose context has a deep symbolic meaning that we have lost in the contemporary world, with the commoditization of the form.

To try and reconnect with this form of thinking is difficult from our modern perspective. There is so much to discover, and a change of attitude makes our experience of the music richer as we realise the composition's depth and the devotion of its composer.

One of the failings of modern communication is the frequent lack of metaphor. When I listen to the early songwriting attempts of people who join me on my courses, their logical, direct, and often cliched lyrics let them down. Good lyrics describe the effect of an emotion, not the feeling itself; they draw comparisons and speak poetically. Religious music expresses passion and devotion by describing the angelic hosts praising God, and, by osmosis, you as the listener feel it in your heart. Sacred music is anything but logical, but it has endured through centuries.

Thought experiment

Listen to some classical music with a new awareness of its deeper dimensions. You do not need to know what it is about; just feel, hear, see, smell, touch, and taste its meaning. You could listen to sacred music or to Holst's 'Planet Suite' and experience something of the profound, its mystery.

Music for healing

"Music was not a luxury in times of epidemic uncertainty - it was a necessity." - Dr Chris Macklin

Music has always been used for healing, whether in the form of chanting or singing a hymn to a god or expressing devotion to a goddess.

Playing music had a unique role during the seventh century BC. When the plague struck Sparta, the poet Thaletus was petitioned to sing hymns. Terpender, another poet, was called upon to sing during an epidemic in Lesbos, and Pythagoras used music as a therapeutic device, playing the lyre to soothe and calm the soul (wiki).

The story of Orpheus and his attempt to bring his love Eurydice back from the underworld speaks to the power of music and song and Orpheus' skill to enchant.

In Europe, entire towns would march, sing, and pray to local saintly icons to fend off the plague.

Musicologist Remi Chui says, "When you are making music, you submit your mind, your body to its regulation.

When you make music with others or even dance, you simultaneously contribute and submit to the larger you of the group" (wiki).

We all know the benefits of music, and there is plenty of anecdotal evidence pointing to its healing qualities. There is also significant evidence of its effectiveness in mental health. In a 'Creative' podcast, Nick Jenkins remarked that music became a lifeline for many people during the lockdown, and it is interesting to hear the songs created in that time.

As a teacher of music who is passionate about its healing qualities, not least from my own experience recovering from various traumatic events, I can vouch for its effectiveness.

Many health giving and healing protocols would not be the same without music. From massage, to meditation, exercise classes, and dance, even stressful situations can be lessened by relaxing music, including examination revision and driving.

There are scientific studies that show that singing, playing, and learning a musical instrument is beneficial to health. However, I want you to look at its effect not just in isolation (the scientific paradigm), but as a link in a chain or - probably better put - as part of an ecosystem.

Music, and the arts in general, have an enhancing effect on us and our lives. I'm not entirely sure how or why this happens, but, from observing its impact, it is evident that it does.

Adding music to one's prescription is very powerful, particularly if the lyrics make you think healthy, robust, loving thoughts. Give it a try; it costs nothing and it has no side effects!

Thought experiment

Write a simple song, whether it be a tune that you can sing or a piece to play with a band or just a friend, and write it with the intention of good health. Phrase it in terms of a positive state that you desire, such as "I am healthy and full of energy" rather than "I am no longer ill" or "My headache has gone."

Play this to yourself every day and see what happens. Then write another one and give it to a friend; spread the love.

Shamanic music

Music from cultures that we can term 'shamanic' (a problematic term) gives us an insight into what music may have been like in its earliest form as a way of communing with the other-than-human world.

Experiencing music from Mongolia and the Amazon gives us an insight into the interaction of ritual and music. It may seem unfamiliar to our Western ears and supposed sensibilities, but we need to attain a perspective that is uncluttered by our conditioning and preconceived notions.

The music of the Amazonian ayahuascos is particularly hypnotic and assists the dreamer to travel astrally under the influence and guidance of a psychedelic brew of specific plants. It is also the song of the plant, and the song that the plant itself has given to the shaman. To grasp the power of this - the song being from a plant and a being in itself - is difficult for us, but I believe that all songs have a spirit, just as all things have in an animist cosmology.

The music of the Mongolian and Steppes peoples serves a similar purpose; to link with the spirits, specifically horse spirits and spirits of the land. These are called in for healing and divination, but again this description falls short, as I am explaining it through a colonial lens. The music and the spirits are much more integrated than this into the life of the people. Explaining it in a rational, left-brained way is out of context and disconnected from the whole.

Their music is a form of communion with the greater world, something that we would have understood in the distant past but which has been lost in the modern age. There may be relics of this still in some hymns, but even these are greatly diminished.

In various 'roots' styles of music, such as samba and reggae, there are solid links to what we may call shamanic music. The call of the conga drum in samba and the clave in bossa nova are evidence of this in its purest form. These patterns were not to be varied because they spoke directly to the spirits. It is only when these ideas are taken and used out of context by others not of this tradition that they are changed; the clave pattern used in jazz bossa is a good example.

The revitalisation of music often draws upon roots styles, and maybe we could view rock and roll and punk in this light, as they seem to be vibes that return musically every 15 or so years.

Thought experiment

Listen to various types of roots and shamanic music. Here is a list to get you started:

- Icaros of the Amazon ayahuascos[2]

- Tuvan throat singing of the Steppes[3]

- Aboriginal music[4]

- Samba conga pattern[5]

- Rastafarian Drummers[6]

Set Point theory

In the 1980s, some scientists described the concept of an equilibrium point to explain how people who diet often return to their original weight after finishing their regime. They coined the term 'Setpoint Theory'; the body seems to have a memory of its weight and returns to it after the diet. This idea was then taken up by others who saw similar things in other areas, such as self-improvement, sports training, and health.

Set Point Theory is something I would like to suggest as a natural phenomenon. A guitar string that is too tight when you detune it will sharpen up again as if trying to return to its sharp status. A slack string will do the opposite, going flat after being tuned.

I also see these points in one's ability to play music, practice, become effective as a professional, focus on something, read music, be creative, etc. We might see these points as our 'comfort zone', but I think the concept of a 'set point' is more organic and not just a state of laziness.

So how do we move the set point? Let us return to the

---

2   https://youtu.be/Vg8qqEzBGbo
3   https://youtu.be/qx8hrhBZJ98
4   https://youtu.be/q7Kbt0YG-6s
5   https://youtu.be/5BvJ6mSes4A
6   https://youtube.com/playlist?list=PLF731536B55F80BBA

example of the guitar string. Putting on a set of classical nylon strings and getting them to settle in tune will take a long time unless you overtighten the string and let it naturally flatten into tune, and if you do this a few times, it will have changed its equilibrium point. Maybe this is an idea for sustained weight loss; go beyond the level you are aiming for and then naturally put weight on to reach your desired goal.

For improved practising, try a week or two of intense study and, when you return to standard life patterns, you will find you have increased your capacity to find time and your inclination to learn..

Can breaking one set point affect another? Can fasting change one's ability to play music? On the face of it, this seems crazy; however, I am not so sure. If you look at it, the mind is causing pattern behaviours in all areas, so changing something radically in one place *could* alter other regions. I am pretty confident that this does indeed happen.

It might explain the effectiveness of ritualistic behaviour, around initiations in particular. For instance, rituals change your mind space, which becomes evident as you participate in one. If you think this is not the case, you have not been through an initiation. Not only do they affect you, but they can also affect other aspects of your life: love, family, jobs, etc. You could undertake fasting *and* extreme practising to break the blocks that control your set point. Maybe overwhelming the mind helps us to make lasting changes, and undoubtedly this is a technique in hypnosis where sensory overload induces trance.

I'm sure this all seems a little bit out there. But in these days of caution and caveats, we need to do something to break out of the iron cage. We need new parameters for the human condition; compassion, responsibility for the environment, and new thinking unfettered by old habits.

Thought experiment

Believe that change is possible. Set a target and then go beyond that target before letting go. See if that settles you back into the target zone.

Spell work

If achieving your new set point means that you can do something new, act as if it is already there; for instance, book the music exam, buy clothes for your new weight or stage clothes for your new stage persona.

Track 6.

SHE'S LEAVING HOME, AT LAST!

Lady luck

"Yes, but is he lucky?" - Napoleon

One of the factors overlooked in the success of musicians is luck.

We do not believe in luck in the way we once did, and this has changed within my lifetime. However, in many interviews that I do for the podcast with successful musicians, it comes up repeatedly; the chance meeting, the odd intervention, the unusual conversation, etc.

I am certain that waiting for luck by sitting at home will not endear her to you but going out courting her does. However inconsistent, Lady Luck seems to play a part in most people's experience of the big break.

There is a quote, "The harder I try, the luckier I get", which I am sure is not quite complete, as it is a bit like saying, "The harder I dig, the more of the world I will see". Maybe it would be better to say, "The more connections I make, the more the doors I open". Developing your contacts and possibilities and then focusing back on the short term (since if you only look at the long-term, you may miss what is right in front of you) may have a positive influence on you becoming lucky.

Is it the chaos of nature that frightens us? Does luck prove that there is anarchy in the universe, disproving the reassuring order of our lives? For some, the universe is an illusion.

Everything is a story, and there are no rules, no scientific laws. The point is, what song do you want to sing? What story do you want to tell about your life? In podcaster Miguel Conner's words, "Write your gospel and live your myth".

Creation myths around the world, including the scientific creation 'explanation', hold that in the beginning, there was disorder, chaos, or nothing, until the word or the happening.

Try replacing 'order' with 'synchronicity', a connecting principle of the universe that may not make sense to our logical minds. Much of the cosmic narrative is illogical, so we like to replace it with order instead of the biodiversity of possibilities. But if we look at nature, we see it everywhere.

Is there a dislike of luck because of the implication of anarchy, which is something that frightens us, making us appear small with no control?

Dr Richard Weisman, who researched luck, found that people who thought themselves lucky and those who believed themselves unlucky lived up to their beliefs.

The quote at the beginning, from Napoleon, was his reply to his officers about promoting someone to the rank of Marshall. Napoleon believed in luck or good fortune, and why would he not, as most soldiers and sailors certainly believe in fate in some form?

So let us do what is necessary to attract luck. We could see when it happened before and give ourselves the same ideas and recreate the favourable conditions at the time. Then, maybe Lady Luck will shine on us again.

Remember, it is not about *why* it works from a psychological perspective. It seems that, for the ones who believe in it, it just does.

Thought experiment

If you do not believe in luck, start! You could create a lucky charm if you want to go down the folk route. Maybe get a rabbit's foot or hagstone or make something into a lucky mascot, like a teddy or a picture.

As lucky things start to happen, thank the charm and develop a relationship. Monitor what happens.

There is scientific evidence for this in the work of Dr Richard Wiseman for those who really need convincing; his books are widely available.

Forget creative card packs - find an old tarot card deck and use it

"There is always a time and place to cut cards with the devil." - The Duke of Wellington

Many card packs for creative thinking are available, often advertised on social media as a crowdsourcing campaign, but you don't need these. The best thing to do, from my experience, is to use tarot cards or just ordinary playing cards.

If the Jungian thing is your jam, the tarot's Major Arcana' are the archetypes, but all you need to do is read what you see in the pictures and tell a story as if you are speaking to children. You will be amazed! Include the colours that the characters are wearing, where they're looking, what they are holding, and the landscape. The telling is all relevant because it's the things that your unconscious is picking up.

The cards have lasted for several hundred years, so in line with Nassim Taleb's 'Lindy effect', they are likely to last for several hundred years more, which is much longer than anything invented more recently by psychologists.

All bright things cast a shadow, so turn the cards' meanings to their opposite. For example, consider the shadow of 'The Lovers' card; what are the bad experiences of life and love, and what is it like to suffer the loss of another that you love deeply? For more troublesome cards like 'The Tower' and 'Death', look for new opportunities from adversity. When you look back, one often sees that significant change and benefit transpires from an unfortunate incident in one's life. If you knew it was coming, you would have avoided it, but those events can act as a catalyst for something better.

Please communicate with your nature's darker side, your shadow self; it is where all of the exciting stuff is. Remember, all things are born from darkness; the seed in the ground, the baby in the womb, and your most interesting thoughts come from the darkest recesses of your mind. For those interested in acting, the best characters are often the ones who are evil and dark, and it is much harder to make a convincing character from somebody who is all goodness and light, unless you are Tom Hanks.

Start with three cards and notice how the cards relate to one another. Do characters on the cards look in a particular direction? What stands out? The things you see are meaningful, and your descriptions are meaningful. Many books written about the cards are based on the tarot's interpretation as written by Crowley, Mathers, or Waite from the Edwardian period. These are typical of the colonialist thinking; trying to link everything back to Egypt or Ancient Greece. Don't worry about all that stuff; just read the pictures - it works so much better.

Thought experiment

Come up with ideas for songs, bands, and projects from the spread of cards. See what you get.

The fool, the trickster, and the musician

In the myth, the trickster moves between the worlds passing knowledge to humans and taking payment for it, sometimes to annoy the gods and test the humans.

I use and teach the cut-up technique for songwriting. For the uninitiated, it looks like cheating; however, this was the technique used by the greatest songwriters in pop music, from Lennon to Bowie, from Bolan to Cobain. I am interested in the idea of the trickster musicians like Bowie and Bolan. Many of the great guitar players like Hendrix had techniques that you could look at as trickery. If you look at technology and what it can do, creating an illusion of sound and vision is itself a form of deception, creating an illusion of complexity.

I have pondered how we are trapped by thinking. Some form of deceit needs to happen to fool us into another mode of thinking. Cut-up is an excellent example of this; we often see cut-up as a series of phrases taken out of context from magazines and newspapers, put together in a random form, which weirdly make sense. However, William S Burroughs did more with the technique, using it to predict the future and curse people and businesses that had upset him.

Any form of non-linear irrational thinking can be cut up. For instance, Burroughs would record the sounds that he heard in the street, taking snippets of conversation and then putting them together out of time. He would also flip between TV channels or radio stations and record the dialogue on an open reel tape player or take parts of pictures and put them together. Any of these techniques are the basis of cut-up. An excellent example of this is the cover of Sgt Pepper, which extensively uses the method.

I was explaining this technique once at a Blues Camp Summer School. Somebody remarked that I had burst his bubble. The illusion of these beautiful songs he had listened to over the years had been some form of fraud.

One of the trickster elements in myth and reality is the strange phenomenon of something unusual happening; there is often an element of fraud that goes with it even when it is not necessary because the event is weird enough in itself. An interesting case in point was the Enfield poltergeist. The event was well documented, but the woman who lived in the house told some untruths, making the whole event look fraudulent. Years later, she tried to explain why she had lied about the story's aspects as if the strangeness of what was happening affected her mind.

A book written about the trickster effect states that truth in these situations becomes very malleable. *The Trickster and the Paranormal* by George Hanson looks at these strange effects and is well worth a read.

One can view cut-up as a fraud and not genius, but I think it best mirrors how the mind comes up with ideas in the first place, splicing and dicing memories to create new things. Could this be how things are, that our mind creates and curates the world to eliminate the weirdness most of the time? Only when the weirdness breaks through the dam wall do we experience things as they are.

I suggest you try it and see what results you get. When I work with this, it seems to put me into a dream experience of thinking, and maybe because the unconscious is unlocked, it gives rise to some extraordinary results. I have often shown the technique at a festival and ended up creating a song that seemed to reference a subject covered in a previous talk that I had not attended!

Whether we look at the artists who have used this technique very successfully as being frauds, cheats, and tricksters or not, they often lived lives that seem very unreal to us in our mundane world. This is one of the artistic consciousness areas that we can quickly obtain by using this simple technique. We are creating strange synchronicities in our rational brain.

Thought experiment

You are a great songwriter. Try the technique after watching my video 'Cut-up for lyrics'[7.]

Wayfinding

"Sometimes, when you lose your way, you find YOURSELF" - Mandy Hale

According to Bill Burnett and Dave Evans, "Wayfinding is the ancient art of figuring out where you are going when you don't know your destination. For

---

7   https://youtu.be/DDg1xam2R-E

wayfinding, you need a compass and a direction. Not a map – a direction". I have found this concept quite helpful ever since I more or less rejected the idea of final destinations, materially and spiritually.

This is a valuable concept when it comes to music writing, because the song knows its destination. It comes with its own directionality, in the form of feelings about what the song expresses. The map of the song's components, chords, melodies, lyrics, etc., is always unclear, at least in the beginning. Rarely does the song leap fully formed from the mind; for me, it's probably only happened about three or four times.

Much of this concept of wayfinding is being brave enough to wander off into the wilderness without your map, and this is something that people who attend songwriting classes find the most difficult. They try to rationalise or make things rhyme, or try to edit or filter as they go, when all that is required is for the raw data to erupt out of nothingness.

The concept of 'nothingness' is difficult for the Western person to understand, but allow it to knock down the house of cards that your intellectual reasoning has constructed and challenge the belief that we are entirely rational.

I have spoken about creating songs or inspiring the work that you do to reduce the intellectual mind's banality. The intellect is excellent as an editor but crap as an artist, so, while rationality is a good servant, it is a terrible master. This is where we've arrived three hundred years after The Enlightenment, which - from a trade description point of view - has to be one of the more disingenuous and misleading terms we have yet invented and which could only arise from colonial thinking. The idea infects most of what we do and think in the West; that we have got the right idea and the planet needs saving by us, when we are the ones that got us into this ecological mess in the first place.

So let the music flow and the ideas develop. When you feel you have arrived at the destination it is time to do a little bit of mapmaking, so that you can discover where your song has arrived, how you got there, and learn more about the final destination. In other words, the editor needs to come in and tidy everything up before you present your song to polite society. But if you don't want to, or feel it stands as is, then leave it be, and people can make of it what they will. People are attracted to mysteries, and letting the listener attempt to solve the clues draws them in further.

Try this as an idea: start with some random lyrics and chords from somewhere, change them around, and allow the song to take its own direction before you attempt to structure the ideas. If the song wants to stay with a set of four chords, then let it. If it wants to become more complicated, let it. In other words, let the song do whatever *it* feels it wants. See how it changes your thinking regarding the 'writing' of music. It is an excellent technique for teaching children, as it demystifies the artistic process (or perhaps re-mystifies it!) and makes it accessible to everybody.

Think of the music as a landscape and see how that translates. How do you navigate the terrain? Feel your way by listening … where does it want to go? What does it make you think of? What pictures, feelings, smells, tastes does it conjure? Allow these to inform and drive the ideas forward. Use them to find your way.

Track 7

THE GENTLEMAN,
FLYING LOW

Bring out the magic in your mind

"Bring out the magic in your mind."

My mother had a book by Al Koran called *Bring Out the Magic in Your Mind,* which came out in the mid-1960s. Al Koran was a mentalist, a bit like Derren Brown is today, and this book (which I still own) links me to my mother's positive thinking ideas, reminding me of the experiments in ESP that she would conduct with me when I was as young as six.

The book is full of examples of acting as if what you wanted had already arrived or was on its way, such as buying carpets for a particular type of car you wanted or getting a door handle for a new house. This type of thinking was very much along the lines of the 'New Thought' movement that was popular in America.

Here's an example from the chapter Magic of Visualisation':

The first step is knowing what you want. Exactly what and when. Want a car? Do you want an old Austin or a brand-new Cadillac? Perhaps it's a Jaguar that you want? Be specific; tell your subconscious in so many words precisely the make and type of car you want and when you want it. The new Jaguar isn't going to do much good when you are on your deathbed. Make it clear what you want and when.

You wouldn't ask for a new Jaguar in five minutes because your intellect would say, "There is no hope of getting such a car in five minutes!" And you wouldn't get it. Be reasonable. Give a sensible time. Now the thing is, you may be unable to see how to get the new Jaguar on what you are earning now, but other factors come into play. You may get a sudden windfall. You may hit the jackpot in some exciting competition. If you do the pools, possibly it's your turn for the big money. Don't draw lines between the possible and the impossible. Leave it to your subconscious to get it for you in its own magical way, by command of your will.

Later, in the next paragraph, he hits the nail on the head concerning the technique, which looks very familiar from a NLP perspective of engaging the senses:

Never for one moment should you limit yourself because you cannot see where such glorious things are coming from. Go and look at the cars, especially the Jaguars, if that is what you want, and feel the joy in your heart. Feeling counts, feeling is the secret. When it comes to control of the subconscious mind, feeling plays a very important part. Feeling that you can get that Jaguar car you want. You're going to enjoy life when you get it. Feel that excitement now; you obtain your desire by feeling like you already got what you want.

See yourself behind the wheel; see yourself driving that wonderful automobile. See it draw up in front of your house. If you do this, if you see that picture, it is bound to materialise. It is the law.

"Screwy, that's what he is, screwy."

No, my friend. To create the magic of visualisation, you must hold the picture clearly in your mind. Every detail of it, see it, feel it, get yourself a scrapbook and paste in images of the things you want, put that Jaguar on the first page. You think it's all nonsense this visualisation? Right, hit the nail on the head with a hammer. It may be called nonsense, but it may nonetheless be true. Behave as though you believe.

Although this book was printed in 1964, the details are almost identical to many bestselling books of recent years.

As I've mentioned before, I think the most exciting thing about this technique is that it is free to do. The only caveat I would add is that action needs to be taken for these things to become possible. Don't expect to win the lottery if you haven't bought a ticket. Don't expect money to come if there isn't a route for it to manifest. Otherwise, it will come in a way you hadn't anticipated, with some ramifications (I can attest to this from my personal experience).

It is also a good idea to enchant for good possibilities and opportunities and allow those routes to open up.

Another great exponent of new thought was Neville Goddard, who Mitch Horowitz has written extensively about in his excellent book *The Miracle Club*. Neville Goddard believed that your imagination was God and therefore you create reality as you exercise your imagination. Neville Goddard was not a name that people remembered until his legacy was resurrected by Mitch's book; however, he profoundly affected many people, including Carlos Castaneda. There is a point of view that Neville's Indian mystic mentor, who may or may not have been real, was an idea that Castaneda adopted with his 'teacher' Don Juan; a literary device to tell his story.

Neville Goddard presented people with a challenge that they would manifest their desires if they used their imagination. He used to say, "Try it, prove me wrong".

But for us creative musicians, we *need* to be imaginative. We need to believe. We need to think that we can succeed against all the odds when the statistics point to other probabilities. We need to believe that what we say or create can be accepted and loved by others.

Neville Goddard started life in a family that was desperately short of money, and he used his ideas to create a successful life for himself against all the odds. Remember that human ideas become real, like law, money, human rights, commerce, and trade. These things did not exist, but somebody had a bright idea and made them real. They all started in the human imagination; someone created them, they then became believable by others using that idea and then became reality.

Thought experiment

Even if you do not believe in the above, the people who rule you do. It reminds me of something that I heard from an astrologer once: "Millionaires don't believe in astrology, but billionaires do".

Remember, these ideas are free; use them.

Imagine, act, and open your mind.

Wisdom in music

"Beloved Pan, and all ye other gods who haunt this place, make me beautiful within and grant that whatever happens outside of me will help my soul grow. May I always be aware that true wealth lies in wisdom, and may my 'gold' be so abundant that only a wise man can lift and carry it away. For me, that is prayer enough." – Socrates

For several years now, I have wrestled with the question, "What direction should my work in music take?" The Internet is awash with people showing you every conceivable guitar solo, song, or technique, and the idea of adding more to this maelstrom of material strikes me as a waste of time.

Nowadays, there are more guitar teachers than people wanting to learn, or it certainly seems that way! What keeps me interested in teaching music is the step beyond the technical song; the stuff that people typically get hooked upon. In other words, it is the wisdom behind it all. What is it that pervades the mind of a great musician? Whether that is Jeff Beck, Jimi Hendrix, Miles Davis, Andre Segovia, Paganini, Johann Sebastian Bach, Art Tatum, or Duke Ellington. What they did is not significant to us, as students, unless we can unpack it; not the knowledge, but the wisdom. The insight can manifest in many ways beyond the song, whereas concentrating on the knowledge does not go as far; it seems to confine us.

This is not a criticism of those other people out there, but more a critique of the way we think. We learn in a way that has been imposed on us by the education system and society at large. We cannot possibly know greatness just by filling our heads with stuff, because doing so fails to answer how we arrive at the 'genius level' (which often happens at a very young age). Notwithstanding the 10,000 hour rule, wisdom is the thing that creates something exciting and new that expresses depth, and this can often happen very early in an artist's career.

At this point, if you are finding it difficult to draw the comparison between knowledge and wisdom, consider this: simply communicated, knowledge tells us that a tomato is a fruit, but wisdom tells us not to put in a fruit salad. Learning music from this perspective of discernment can give us great insights into the musician and their art form. Knowledge and technique are purely a toolkit to express it, and this is where practice comes in, to develop that toolkit.

Socrates states another good point here: he refers to wanting to be beautiful *within* and for the gods to grant whatever needs to happen outside to help that interiority grow. That interiority is where wisdom resides.

How often do you hear someone on the Internet say, "What was Hendrix feeling here? What inner sounds was he hearing?" Because something *was* going on, and if we can only get a whiff of it, it will transform one's playing. We will not necessarily sound like the person we are modelling with that information, but - better still - we will sound like ourselves.

Thought experiment

Ask questions. How did Eddie Van Halen come up with his tapping style? What was the motivation for reinvention that musicians like David Bowie or Miles Davis had?

The answer is not important, but where the question takes you is.

See if it changes your ideas in any way. Keep the mystery there, as wisdom keeps that intact, whereas finding the answer does not.

Sometimes sticking the word 'maybe' in front of the response to a question helps. For instance, "Maybe Bowie's belief in characters in drama and art drove his creativity".

Become wise.

Trees and hedgerows and their significance to artistic thinking

I have a friend involved with the Wildlife Trust in Kent, and we were discussing the rationale behind taking out old hedgerows and the subsequent effects on topsoil erosion (as you do). The economic argument behind doing this is that you can use machinery and make the work more effective if a field is more extensive. However, we discovered the long-term effect is detrimental; a little bit like killing the goose that lays the golden egg - you may get a short-term benefit for a long-term disaster.

I grew up in Cornwall, and I met some old farm labourers who lived and worked on the land and had some old-time wisdom that often features in West Country jokes. One of these is about a guy who turns up in a flash car and asks directions from an old farmer: "What's the quickest way to get to Scotland from here?" The farmer thinks for a while and says, "Best not to start from here." This sums up the problem that we have currently. Many things, including the education system, health care, and the environment, are best fixed someplace other than where we are.

There were cases around the time of the Enclosure Acts in which trees that had played a role in generations of a family became the possession of the landowner who took control of the common land. This was one of the most effective and devastating forms of theft that we ever experienced in this country, but it is rarely taught in any meaningful way in schools. The people with money stole the land from the poor by changing the law, and they disenfranchised ordinary people like you and me.

Old-style thinking was that a tree that lived on the land did not belong to anyone; it belonged to that place. Now, this argument works incredibly well when it comes to environmental thinking. If that tree has a right to exist and has some form of ownership of the land on which it sits, then by keeping it, the tree effectively safeguards all of the environmental infrastructures it supports and is supported by. A simple way of expressing a complex idea, just like listening in your head to the melody and playing it, is more straightforward than explaining how the music works theoretically.

The intellectual approach is too simplistic and inefficient when dealing with complex environments and musical expression. A hedgerow creates incredible diversity. Diversity increases in areas bordering something else, such as a shoreline, forest edge, or - in this case - the edge of a field. It is also a way of looking at music that does not sit easily within a genre, in that it might create more musical biodiversity. The Beatles and their use of Indian music is an example.

So there we have it! Music and hedgerows, and we have not even got into the song of the Blackbird and Thrush, which, along with the Oak, Hawthorn, and Apple, would give us plenty of material in the English folk music tradition.

Thought experiment

We can easily miss the importance of this type of thinking, but it situates the song in a place and a time, embodying it. If we include something of the here and now, such as a real place, it creates a powerful effect. I have heard storytellers do this with ancient tales, and it connects you directly to the narrative.

So experiment with creating a piece that talks of something in your environment. That could be a favourite tree, hill, flower, a crossroads, or - if you live in a city - a building, a river, or a high street.

You may, as you read this, think of songs that do that. There are lots of them, such as 'Route 66', 'London's Calling', and 'Solsbury Hill'.

THE INSIDER

Under the thin veneer of respectability there is a wild animal

"Music expresses that which cannot be put into words and that which cannot remain silent." - Victor Hugo

We are still the same creation throughout time and in all races. Scratch the surface and we are wild animals stimulated by the same passions, feelings, and instincts as our brothers and sisters in the animal world.

The parts of the brain that kick in when there we perceive a threat are the same as for any other creature. We share a compulsion to survive and protect our loved ones. There may be some who have rewired themselves, but only very few. This similarity gives us a way of understanding ourselves just by looking at nature.

Language is powerful, not because of the rational meanings of words but because of the reactions they can trigger. Look at how language has been used on you to sell.

Something that makes you feel uncomfortable, worried, or frightened can then be worked on to dig deeper, and then there is the offer of a solution. The feeling of protection and confidence, and all you need to do is sign on the dotted line and buy the product.

The psychology of salesmanship is so good that they can play you like a musical instrument, and they know exactly which keys to push. They know how to future pace your objections and then disarm you.

In recent times I have watched the news about Covid-19 and seen how the news was geared towards a particular narrative. Now, I'm not saying that it isn't a good idea to receive this information, but building fear from raw numbers of Covid deaths without comparing them to anything can lead to the same sort of vulnerability. Where is the comparison to regular numbers of fatalities in the same period? What happened to the numbers of people dying of cancer, heart disease, and road accidents?

Any set of numbers for an entire population are by their very nature large and, by extension, misleading if not placed in their proper context.

Another point that I am particularly interested in is the prevalence of mental illness and depression. Where is the reporting of this? Because it is a massive issue.

Life is terminal. To regain strength, we need to reconnect with the resources that we have as humans. To connect with the power that we have as creatures of the earth.

Be brave, courageous, loving, and helpful. We are community creatures; we need others. Look at what happened as a result; people dying alone was not what human creatures do as communal beings.

Make music like birds. Make art and dance with others. We are ritual makers, pattern seekers, the creature who sings to the stars and howls at the moon.

Thought experiment

What would your music look like if it was wild and powerful?

Since you are full of courage, what would it sound like if you created it while being off your face, drunk, or danced to exhaustion, in a rage and impassioned?

'Swish' ... it has gone, replaced by the better you

Much of what we believe we can and can't do is learned behaviour.

Some of these things can be changed very rapidly by a NLP technique called 'Swish'.

Let's say that you have a problem with spiders and find them frightening; even the smallest one can set you up with a fear response that is irrational but profound.

The first thing that you need to do is to picture the spider and experience its associated feelings. Picture it, feel the emotions, and hear your inner dialogue. Experience it in as vivid an amount of detail as possible. See where the picture is placed in your imagination. Do you see that in front of you? Is it in colour? What feelings has it tapped into? Then come out of that experience.

This time create a new picture, have a friendly spider, something comical wearing a party hat, roller-skates, and blowing a party hooter.

Contrast the two pictures. If the frightening one was dark and gloomy, make the other one bright and shiny. Really work on the second picture, make it positive, enchanting, anything that responds to the positive aspects of who you are.

Return to your original picture, drain out the emotional aspects, lessen the image, turn down the colour, or add colour if that helps you?

To create a break, think of something entirely different for a moment, then go back to the original drained picture and suddenly, with a swishing sound, swap it for the nicer, fun, colourful, good feeling picture of the spider.

It might help you to shrink the first picture as you switch it and exchange it for the big bright, happy image. Make a swishing sound as you do this, as if it has been blown away or transformed by a machine.

Making the switch as theatrical as possible makes a big difference, because we deal with aspects of the mind that like presentation, making it fun, colourful, and exciting.

I've used several variations of this technique, including a woman doing training for her women's group. I helped her to visualise a makeup compact with a mirror that switched the original image on one side and the new one on the other, and it proved very effective for her.

Try it as an imaginary video on an internal film screen. The first picture of you onstage suffering from stage fright is grainy and flickering, but then it swishes to the confident you onstage, really owning the space. Then embody the feeling of standing, looking out into the audience, holding the space in real life.

Interestingly, change really can happen that quickly. I often explore the phobias that people suffer. They never practised having a phobia, it is something that they learnt very quickly, but it never fails to kick in. It would be fantastic if we could learn everything so quickly. I suppose in many ways we could, if we could achieve that emotional impact.

Thought experiment

Take something that is bothering you and go through the above actions; take the original picture, drain the emotions, sound, and feeling.

Build a better picture with the outcome that you require, even using an example of what you would do if that problem didn't exist anymore, feeling full of life happiness with all the positive attributes you would like to put into your life. Make one magically disappear as the other comes in and make a loud swishing noise or fanfare noise or imagine car horns with flashy lights. SSSSSSWIIIIIISSSHHHHHHHH.

Then move away from the idea, think of something else, and then return to test that you've got the new emotional information. Repeat as necessary or as required.

No explanation, just an acceptance of unconscious understanding

"The curse of modernity is that we are increasingly populated by a class of people who are better at explaining than understanding." - Nassim Taleb

I recently finished the eleventh year of Blues Camp, and - as usual - the playing and songwriting from the campers was amazing. Each year seems to get better. All we do is let people create; however, that is often easier said than done. It takes some psychological trickery for people to feel empowered to be open and creative. Several times, we will see individuals close down by reverting to the default rational thinking, even though they are told that is not where musical creativity originates. If that were true, they would already be creative.

I have learned over the years that people fear change to their beliefs. This is why someone will come for coaching but will fight against the change that starts to happen within them. There is a difficulty in realising that, deep down, what they believe is not valid. This can be explained through maths, and I will hand it over to Lionel Snell to put it more eloquently:

"The rational view of the world is ultimately a logical one. To admit one little miracle or inconsistency into a logical system is not as harmless as you might think. It causes complete disruption.

"An example of such a logical system is arithmetic. If we obey all the rules of arithmetic but allow just one wrong result, then any wrong result can be proved. Let us say that we allow 5 + 7 = 10, therefore 12 = 10, therefore 12 - 10 = 0, therefore 2 = 0. Divide both sides by 2 and you get 1 = 0. This means that all numbers are now equal to 0 (e.g., multiply both sides by one hundred to get one hundred equals zero). Therefore all numbers are equal to each other. In other words, the whole of arithmetic collapses if we admit one single illogical result into the system.

"So when something appears to be an inconsistency, the rational mind will take great pains to avoid confrontation with the miraculous. It's not awkward or deceptive; it is defending the conscious form from chaos."

Often people will come up with the phrase, "scientists have discovered" or "it has been proven scientifically that", but frequently such claims are not valid. Science is a method, a system, a tool, not a philosophy. Therefore, the tool to do a job is occasionally (perhaps more often than we might realise) the wrong tool for the job, particularly when we come to the area of creative thought. Creativity seems to be inhibited by the rational, leading to writers' block, stage fright, etc. So give your analytical thinking a break for a while and enter into some unfettered creative thinking. No explaining, no limits; in fact, endless possibilities. Bend and warp reality and see what you come up with. No explaining, just an acceptance of unconscious understanding.

You want it darker?

"You want it darker?" - Leonard Cohen

Okay, let's go darker, let us plumb the depths. We danced with your shadow and fed the demons, now let us go and feast with them and invite them for a holiday. Let us look at how music stirs up the shadow side of the human condition, which is to the right of Genghis Khan and would embarrass the Marquis de Sade.

Invoking said spirits and demons might be a way of changing one's reference point or set point.

There is much to be said about the fact that there is an equilibrium or set point in our health, wealth, and wellbeing, whether it be a social or financial situation to which we find ourselves returning. It is often similar to our parents' income, health, and luck. So how do we change that equilibrium point? Read the chapter on 'Set Point theory'.

So here is where the darkness comes in. Take yourself to a place that frightens you, saddens you. Do a survival course that pushes you to the edge. Do a marathon. Maybe the Christian idea of giving everything away is more to do with this than charity. You break the set point by moving to the extreme of what you are looking to build, the new equilibrium nearer to your goal.

Let us apply this to music. Maybe to succeed in something new, something more compelling, more powerful, sexy, passionate, or compassionate, you should become the embodiment of what you want and push it further. If you're going to become the Mystic, then fast in the wilderness.

Write a song about your intention that you find challenging to put out there. Express your greatest fears, or anger, greed, or loss, and put them into a song.

Here are some examples: Black Sabbath, Bowie, and Iggy Pop. And in the arts, we have Salvador Dali, and Picasso, and in literature, William S.Burroughs and Philip K Dick.

Leonard Cohen took himself and his band to the limits of intoxication but later became a Zen monk before returning to music before he died.

So the question is, how brave are you? And how much change do you want to make in your life and the world?

Thought experiment

This one I leave to you. Push the boundaries of your comfort zone. Your life is your responsibility, not someone else's. One of the problems we face today is that few people have autonomy, and loss of autonomy leads to depression in the workplace. So visit the darkness. Take a lesson from mythology and leave a thread so that you can return after slaying the Minotaur in the labyrinth.

The fool, the trickster, and the musician

In the myth, the trickster moves between the worlds, passing knowledge to humans and taking payment for it, sometimes to annoy the gods and test the humans. Even if this seems to be a repetition of an event, perhaps it bears repeating.

I am interested in the idea of the trickster musicians like Bowie and Bolan. Many of the great guitar players, like Hendrix, had techniques that you could look at as trickery. If you look at technology and what it can do, creating an illusion of sound and vision is itself a form of deception, creating an illusion of complexity, or even a similarity to something that went before.

I have pondered how we are trapped by thinking. Some form of deceit needs to happen to fool us into another mode of thinking. Cut-up is an excellent example of this; we often see cut-up as a series of phrases taken out of context from magazines and newspapers, put together in a random form, which weirdly make sense. However, William S Burroughs did more with the technique, using it to predict the future and curse people and businesses that had upset him.

Any form of non-linear irrational thinking can be cut up. For instance, Burroughs would record the sounds that he heard in the street, taking snippets of conversation and then putting them together out of time. A repetition of something that happened before, but which is repeated at a later date, can have unusual effects.

Thought experiment

Experiment with repetition.

Or experiment with repetition.

CHRIST, I'M SIXTY-FOUR!

The search for perfection and technical brilliance? Don't.

Why is it that the most remarkable artists are always flawed? Johnny Cash, Jimi Hendrix, Jim Morrison, Janis Joplin, to name just a few. The performances from these were far from perfect. In fact, they teetered on the edge of disaster most of the time, such as the concerts of Amy Winehouse.

What is it that we are missing here? These people seemed to thrive on being on the edge. Is that the key that we seem to be missing here, by approaching their ability intellectually? We have a conception that makes us strive for perfection, yet the reverse seems to hold a secret, and I think we know this deep down; otherwise, we would not be as captivated by the failings of the masters.

Were the personal demons of these artists the things that drove them and made them so captivating? As a thought experiment, let us imagine that they were, and let us take our psychological shadows for a walk.

There is a Buddhist concept, which I believe comes from Tibetan Buddhism, of feeding your demons. Invoking them, getting to know them, and then providing for them helps you bring them into your mind. They need feeding anyway, and if ignored, they will disrupt your life, as well as feed off you, so bring them in! I choose to consider them as builders and labourers doing work for you. Make sure you pay them and treat them with respect, and do not ignore their payment requests. This is covered in Aidan Wachter's book *Six Ways*.

I suggest you get his book because it's full of marvellous ideas, and he describes this technique better than I do.

But just to precis his idea, you need to take two chairs or two cushions and set them facing one another. You sit in one and invite your demon to sit in the other. Allow time for this and talk to him/her for a while just as you would another person, then ask who they are and what they need. Then sit in its place; feel, hear, and assume the form of the entity. Let it speak through you, then change seats and speak as yourself, and repeat.

You will find out why it is there and what it needs from you to become one of your allies. If you are patient enough and talk well, you will find this a helpful communication, and remember, that word has the same root as 'to commune'.

I am aware that some people's demons are very much in the driver's seat, and they think that - as the host - such a person will be unaware of it. Their world view is that of the controlling (put whatever you want in here) demon/entity/emotion/mental viewpoint/disturbance.

In this case, it will probably mean that such a person would not do this exercise, as they are not in the driver seat, and why would such a thing want to lose control?

Our failings and inadequacies are essential; use them to your advantage. Hendrix was not the best guitarist technically for his time, not by a long shot, but he touched more people than any other guitarist, and his performances, although flawed, were entrancing.

Instead of looking for perfection and dancing in the light, step into the shadows and dance. Invite the parts of you that you do not like, be it your character flaws - anger, jealousy, greed - or your ability flaws - lack of patience, heavy-handedness, inaccurate playing - and let them join the feast. See what they bring to the party. Stop pretending to be someone else. Stop being the shop front that you show the world, and bring the workers out from the backroom. Do what Freddie Mercury did; lay it out for all to see, but in your own way, and see what happens.

Your demons may have some cool tricks up their sleeves. Let's face it; they have had to put up with you all these years!

Happiness is the absence of striving for happiness

I like paradoxes, as they contain truth. Every light casts a shadow, and we do not care too much for the darkness of things, but often the darkness gives us the true meaning of their essence. How true is this with music? How many great songs are written by people who are not particularly significant on the instruments they play? For many, being a great player is a drawback for a writer, with only a few exceptions, such as Hendrix and Clapton.

To succeed, don't try to. When you give up measuring yourself by your markers of success, it flows more freely. Something understood by entrepreneurs is that money is a marker, not the end goal. Often the plan will be something less obvious, like the challenge of making something happen or what success enables you to achieve.

It is better to focus the mind on things that success would afford you, instead of the victory itself. Rather than the pupil and teacher focusing on the grade, imagine what the achievement will enable you to do? Seeing yourself playing in a band that performs a particular style of music that requires a level of knowledge is a better motivator than focusing on the examination day and the piece of paper you receive at the end of it.

The mind seems to have a way of flagging up possibilities of acquiring the ways and means of achieving that possibility. I often use the story of buying a new car; once you have decided on which model and which colour you will buy, one starts to see that colour and that model everywhere. We are alert to the possibilities of acquiring that which we desire.

Thought experiment

Once we have a belief system, the unconscious will find evidence of the truth of that belief in the world around us. Now, if we take this as a fact for the time being, it means that things that appear to be wholly accurate might be just a fabrication of how we think. Let us use this to believe something different, something better. See what happens. Be observant to possibilities that come your way.

Now take those things as a flow of possibilities. Don't grasp at them but let them come to you. See if that changes your 'normal'. Often, the desire for something shows its lack in your life, and that might be holding you back.

So back to happiness: by searching out the result of joy - such as being with friends, having connections with family, the feeling of support and assistance - this is where one can find happiness.

Success with music is giving success to others, and happiness can be found by providing satisfaction to others.

Internal studio

When I was 16, I travelled to Newcastle to attend a seminar with the jazz guitarist Barney Kessel.

Kessel was one of the great guitar players of the 20th century. Not only was he a great player, but he was a master of musical psychological playing, and many of his ideas I now equate with the early days of NLP.

However, I will focus here on one of the many anecdotes that he told. Kessel knew Django Reinhardt, Stefan Grappelli, Oscar Peterson, and Count Basie and had collaborated with many, including Billie Holiday and Ellie Fitzgerald, but the story he told concerned Louis Armstrong.

Louis was a superstar, and he was flown all over the United States to play various cities. Each gig was with a different band who he had not seen until the day of the concert.

Someone asked Louis how he was consistently on form, even though some of the musicians he was working with were not top rate.

His answer was priceless and very revealing. He said, "I have a rhythm section that I hear in my head, and I listen to them unless the guys out there are better."

One of the skills of a creative is the internalisation of sound or picture; the internal studio or concert hall is where it all happens before it merges into the world.

Developing this ability from the outset - playing the

music in your head, seeing the picture, or feeling the dance - is the way to make this happen. The skill is strengthened by blending the senses together, so see the music or the music video, hear the piece that goes with the story, and smell the cooking in the village that the classical guitar music is coming from as you see grandma cooking the paella in an old Spanish town.

Music is rooted in the senses, not in the intellect. You cannot play or sing if it's only in your head as an intellectual thought. Your soul is not in your head.

Barney Kessel went on to talk about how he heard his guitar. He said it was The Count Basie Big-Band, and he demonstrated it by playing the blues, at first mimicking the trumpets, the saxophones, and then the double bass. It reminded me of Andrea Segovia, the master of the classical guitar, who said his guitar was an orchestra.

I can also see that type of thinking in Jimi Hendrix's playing, for his favourite chord was a staple of a horn section, the riffs sounded like a sax, and Jimi bounced between them.

Thought experiment

When you practice and play, make sure you listen and make the creative changes in your imagination. The idea is for it to appear internally and not to originate in the intellect.

If you think you cannot do this, think of a melody that you know well, such as 'Happy Birthday', and, after hearing it in your head, change the instrumentation so that you're hearing it played on the trumpet. That is it; it's as simple as that.

What can we learn from ecosystems?

If you look at ecosystems, they are highly complex, diverse, and seemingly full of conflict; however, we are beginning to see that this apparent conflict creates a self-organising, self-balancing system.

In contrast, when we create systems, we often end up in a place where everything is predicated on one or two points. An excellent example of this is the Global Positioning System (GPS), on which so many systems are dependent, including traffic, financial systems, air-traffic control, and many others. If the system goes down, we have a real problem.

So let's have a look at what we can do artistically by modelling an ecosystem. Let's take your back garden.

A healthy ecosystem will have everything you love in the garden and all the things you hate. There will be ants, slugs, blackfly, greenfly, a few mice, and most definitely a rat or two running around.

You will also have the things that you like; the bees, butterflies, and - if you're lucky - the plants that you want. But, inevitably, the more you try to exclude the things that you don't like and focus on the things that you do like, the more the plants become prone to funguses and microbes.

Songbirds and predatory wasps depend upon the things that we consider pests. Hedgehogs eat slugs. Unfortunately, if you've poisoned the slugs with pellets, you will probably kill the hedgehog as well.

In an interview with Stephen Fry and Jordan Peterson, Stephen Fry gave an example from a psychologist who demonstrated that natural randomness compares to human logical thinking. Fry suggested that if we had a piece of perspex floating on water on which lots of mice were running around, because of the randomness of their activity, it would remain stable. However, if you did the same thing with a suitably sized piece of perspex and put humans on it, the fact that they planned for people to stand in particular places would result in it capsizing and everybody ending up in the water.

I think this is a perfect analogy to the situations that we often find ourselves in. We are sitting on numerous time bombs that are ticking away, whether that be the financial system or how global capitalism seems to be consuming all available resources. The impending ecological disaster we are watching unfold. Then there is Covid and many other problems. A one-size-fits-all scenario does not work.

So let's draw a comparison to music. Generally speaking, when people start, they like to learn something in the way that they assume it should be done, by following the rules. However, the most memorable and successful artists never follow the rules. They break, bend, distort, and put things together that shouldn't go together, like your wasps in the garden and your bees, the things you like and the things you do not want. They create tension; they shock, act in ways that revolt people, and yet the very fact that they do these things makes them successful.

Another point to consider here is that artists' best work often comes at a point in their lives when they've got everything to lose and are virtually starving. It is challenging for an artist to continue that level of productivity and creativity when they start to have enough to feed themselves and live a comfortable life.

There seems to be something baked into nature that requires the good and the bad to coexist. The thing that we like and the thing that we don't like conflict with our desire for comfort and sustenance and for everything to be safe.

From a psychological perspective, going out and observing the square foot of ground in your garden may be one of the best lessons for creativity that you're likely to find. There is something intense and meaningful in how the creatures - the hunters and the hunted - live virtually side-by-side in that tiny bit of ground. We need to be more eco-minded in our thinking and creativity.

Thought experiment

Spend some time in nature. Go to places that challenge you. Spend some nights in a small tent in the middle of nowhere.

See how little you can live on and - if you can forage - use that to augment your food.

Watch what nature does and make notes. See what creative ideas come to you. I can assure you that when you get hungry, you get great ideas.

Track 10

PEARL OF ENDEARMENT

Set fire to the world

"I have only one and ancient desire, let me stand next to your fire" - Jimi Hendrix

What is needed to start a fire? Dry kindling, followed by dry wood of suitable size - starting small and then gradually getting larger, up to the largest logs - plus of course something to create the initial spark. Once alight, the fire needs to be fed and watched over.

A sequence usually occurs when lighting a fire. Plenty of preparation and some ability to set it alight, including positive actions to nurture it. Something else worth considering is what the fire is intended to do. Is it to keep you warm, to cook with, or something else? This will affect the way that the fire is constructed and where. Let us adopt this metaphor and 'set fire to the world' or consider 'fire in the head', the old term for inspiration.

I find it interesting that these terms explain what is required to be successful with artistic endeavours. If the ground is not ready for the fire to be lit, you will not be successful. The territory requires preparation for the type of music you have. Sufficient tinder is needed to get started and for enough fuel to build the fire.

The world might be ready for you, but nothing will happen if you do not create the spark. Interestingly enough, many fire lighting skills require you to blow and breathe at various stages to feed the fire. We can draw an analogy here to marketing and speaking about your product, such as being interviewed on radio, TV, and the Internet. Maybe you need to say something incendiary!

It's easy to miss how we have been prepared by music courses and the curated fantasy of programs like 'The Voice' and 'The X Factor' to think that we can just go on and play or perform, as in some form of circus. This might be the route for a very small number of people, but I find it interesting that the most significant artists, such as Adele, Ed Sheeran, and Amy Winehouse, did not take this path. Adele started out on the road to success with a profile on Myspace (remember that?), picked up small gigs, gained exposure on radio and TV, and often went out with a single guitarist to perform intimate shows.

We can take the fire metaphor as far as we want, because it can also lead to burnout. Most fires do eventually burn out and need to be rebuilt, and to some extent, that is what Adele did in between her various albums. Maybe thinking about success strategies is better for artistic people, because there is a feeling to it that intrinsically makes sense. Many marketing systems are so 'in your head' - being dry and expressionless - that they are difficult to feel your way through. Something that incorporates an elemental force, such as fire, is much easier for us to envisage and taps into our creativity at a fundamental level.

I do not wish to imply that everyone should be aiming for world domination. Your target could be something simpler, like developing your teaching level, moving into a new area of work, or just building up the numbers of people having lessons. Just try it out and see how you get on - I will watch out for smoke on the horizon.

Thought experiment

Learn how to make fire properly. The best way is to seek out someone who teaches it and be there with them in person, because there seems to be some form of transference.

Once you can make fire, you can embody it and use its essence in your work; remember, creativity is 'fire in the head'.

A couple of links for you:

- Ruby Taylor teaches fire making on a number of her courses, and I interviewed her for my 'Creative' podcast[8.] For further details, see her website 'Native Hands'[9.]

- For more about Adele's rise to fame (or should I say flame, and maybe this chapter should have been called 'Set Fire to the Rain'), listen to my interview with her guitarist Ben Thomas[10.]

I have done the workshop, now unleash me on the world

"The fool doth think himself wise, but the wise man knows himself to be a fool" - William Shakespeare

From years of teaching and being involved in NLP, I have come to realise that part of the problem is the 'weekend workshop'. My fascination with the mind and consciousness

---

8   Creative, Jan 20th, 2021, https://www.listennotes.com/podcasts/creative/ruby-taylor-ltBhe7zInwY/
9   https://nativehands.co.uk/
10 Creative, Nov 5th, 2019, https://www.listennotes.com/podcasts/creative/ben-thomas-AFdXWYZ02Pg/

has led to me exploring many things - music, hypnosis, meditation - and all of these have fed into my work. I have seen the rise of the workshop and seminar course to a level that did not exist even a few years ago in this country. There are workshops for everything - hot yoga, raw food, Tantric techniques - and all of this is driven by the desire of somebody to sell something.

An unintended consequence is that someone attends a weekend workshop and instantly becomes a practitioner. This is not to say that I think that university courses on alternative topics are any better than herbalism courses that do not involve going out and actually finding the plants in the wild. There are massage courses that do not include physical contact (I kid you not!) and music courses that do not teach you how to make money; both leave you to learn this by chance, it appears. Obviously, in the past, if you wanted to use herbs you literally learnt in the field. The herbalists of old never studied their craft in a formal setting, so they never got trapped in a data-driven intellectual perspective. Much of the data and statistics are - at best - misinterpretations and – at worst - literally pulled out of thin air. We have all seen data that supports one interpretation but is later refuted by other data. The thing that seems to be missing is personal experience, and there is a difference between gathering data and reading it.

So how does the teaching of music fit into this? Music was once the domain of the amateur; people learnt by watching a master and experimenting on their own and sometimes by being apprenticed to another musician. Once the church got involved and music became codified, a pattern developed such that musicians learned to play from a script of written music, devoid of some of its essence, and improvisation fell out of favour. Contemporary music in this country conformed, until recently, to the former description, of learning on the job. Now it is learnt in a college setting, and it has all the hallmarks of what I was describing earlier; something disjointed and removed from the root of the music.

So, what to do? Attending the workshop is okay, however, it is only the beginning of a long journey. The temptation to 'evangelise your enlightenment' needs to be repressed for years to develop and mellow the fruit. This will eventually come, long after the seminar's flowering and the college buds have fallen, once the developing fruit has withstood the rain, pests, the wind, and all the interested birds of life that seek to pick at your ideas and resolve.

The resulting distorted and damaged fruits no longer look like the shiny images that the workshop advertising first enticed you with. But they will be hardier and more nourishing and better than anything that the workshop alone afforded you. And how long does it take for this fruit to develop? 10,000 hours …

Observe how a tree grows near the coast, bending away from the prevailing wind coming in from the sea, or a tree on the high downs, which is short but stout; theirs was a process of growth that adapted to the pressures they have experienced, and they are no less beautiful for it.

Learning a skill is the same; practice daily, and over time it will make you into what you do, be it an artist, musician, or athlete.

Thought experiment

Regularly practice to 'become what you do'. This could be general, like a musician or - more specifically - a guitarist or

- more focused still - a classical guitarist concentrating on the compositions of Villa Lobos.

The thing to do is to do the thing. No targets to reach, no grand plan, just steady repetitions of what you want. Walk the path. Grow like the tree blown by the wind to face inland.

What if?

What if the things that you believe are not true? The stories that we currently accept need challenging.

Look at what *you* believe in and what society thinks. What about the things that in the past were held to be true? Some abhorrent ideas were once enshrined in law, such as slavery, the supposed superiority of white people to black people, discrimination against Jews, homosexuality being a mortal sin, etc. We could also add to this list the 'divine right' of kings, the patriarchy, definitions of what constitutes 'heresy' according to the Church, the tenets of Fascism and Communism, etc. Many commonly held ideas are not only profoundly flawed at best, but capable of great evil at worst.

No one should believe that we've got it right now, as there is absolutely no precedent for that. Let's challenge the concept of 'the law'. People who commit crimes may be wired that way. The poor are in poverty because of circumstances created by their ancestors' society, reinforced through successive generations. The law exists to protect those with power to keep their power.

So what about your beliefs and the things and people that you think you can trust? What if it's all just an illusion and you wake up a different person one day? This does of course happen. You are literally a different person; your body is continually becoming something else.

This breakdown or bending of whatever constitutes 'reality' can cause mental illness, but what if it is not an illness, but a reaction to our social environment.

In his book *The Wisdom of Mental Illness*, Jez Hughes discusses this viewpoint. It seems that many conditions may be a reaction to the pressures of society and how humans cope with those stresses. Jez suggests that it could be a way of culture adjusting to changing paradigms, with sensitive people acting as lightning rods. His argument is compelling, particularly when he compares Western and indigenous cultural views of 'mental illness'. In the latter, it is what marks out the shaman to his or her community.

The shaman uses their experience of altered states to help others navigate and negotiate between the world of the spirits and people's perception of reality, after they have come back from what we would term a 'psychotic event'.

If we look at Western society and the destruction that it has caused, can we honestly say that they are wrong and we have it exactly right? We have to make a realistic re-evaluation of what we believe and the outcomes that those beliefs cause. However, when you look at what seems obvious to one person, such as ecological degradation, someone else will argue that it is not happening. Even something as apparent as species loss, which seems obvious to me, is countered by other people claiming there is more diversity.

If we reach a point where we do not know what to believe in anymore, counter-intuitively, it can present possibilities that can be beneficial. It is undoubtedly a more creative space to inhabit because it is less restricted. However, it is a dangerous road, but you are brave, aren't you? May you believe in that which makes you strong.

Thought experiment

For the next few days, change what you believe. Act differently because of this and see where it takes you. As a safety caveat: do no harm and don't be a dick.

Adopt the idea that "Nothing is true, all things are possible".

Change your life ...

KALIMERA!

Playing the guitar is a beautiful thing

Playing the guitar is a beautiful thing, but some people can make it boring or, worse, a misery, and that does take some doing.

An ex-pupil who had just received his music degree contacted me with the following message:

"Uni was good apart from my guitar lessons, sadly. The man who 'taught me' showed me how much a teacher could affect your enjoyment of music! So if I didn't seem grateful at the time, thank you! Because your lessons probably got me through my performance module."

I have always been aware of the teachers who have the unique gift of making the guitar dull. There are many reasons for this. The assumption that the guitar should be taught like a classical instrument is one of them. No offence intended - if you are learning classical guitar, that is a different matter altogether! - but if you are learning a contemporary form of guitar playing, it's not the way to do it.

I see this thinking a lot amongst guitar teachers - that there is a correct way to do something - but this is only the case if you are learning a strict discipline of playing a classical instrument. Still, if you find yourself in this situation, once you get outside the confines and strictures of such a rigid way of thinking, your excitement and capacity to learn will increase.

Remember that all of the great contemporary players had a distinctive way of delivering music. Hendrix played with his teeth, Jeff Healey played the guitar on his lap, Keith Richards adopted a different tuning, and Eric Clapton played so loud that his amp was always on the brink of blowing up. None of them followed the 'correct' technique, with the thumb at the back of the neck and the hand correctly placed over the strings; they all broke the rules.

So what is it that we need to do? I would suggest that a good teacher is an alchemist who works with the ingredients available within the pupil. By mixing these with the elements that the teacher brings, something transformational can be synthesised. There is no way to know what the pupil is capable of, but it is likely to be something entirely beyond what you believe is possible. This has often been my experience; if I allow students to push my ideas beyond my comfort zone, something unique often happens.

Education has sadly become much less about opening the mind and much more about social management and box ticking. Teachers and examinations focus on tempo and technicality when these things are taken in their stride by the pupil that is excited about the prospect of discovering how brilliant they are when being creative.

Because education, and Higher Education in particular, is all about the dollar. It has become an economic machine that needs to be fed, creating more in its own likeness. It is very different from opening the mind like a parachute to explore the creative landscape from a distance while still infused with the excitement of the jump.

So think about what makes music exciting for you, ditch all the stuff you found boring and go for it. As a teacher, only provide technical material that students are desperate to learn.

Thought experiment

Imagine that you have never seen a guitar before. What would you do with it? Maybe you would put it on your lap. What happens with those tuning pegs? Perhaps they are part of how the guitar plays. With what do you play?

Remember that the best keys for the guitar are the ones that feature the open strings; therefore, guitar music is often in the keys of E, A, D, and G. Use the open strings more!

HAVE FUN AND KICK ASS!

Three is a magical number

"Hip hooray, three cheers for Uncle Charlie!"

Everything comes in threes, including magic numbers. Something is hidden in plain sight. Doing something three times seems to encode it into your memory.

I've used this technique in my teaching for years now; getting students to play something three times, and they've got it. It seems to create a neural pathway. Then you can move on and play the following phrase three times, and so on.

Using three senses stacked will also help, so for instance: what do you see, what do you hear, what do you feel? What does it taste like? How does it smell?

The power of three comes up again and again. It comes up in rhetoric; repeating something three times. It comes up in pop songs, with the three-chord trick. It comes up in harmony: we need three notes to create a chord.

We also have the three wise men. We even have three Marys in the Bible. We have the three Norns in Norse mythology, and we have the three witches in Shakespeare's *Macbeth,* and of course we have the Holy Trinity.

Does this speak to us about the structure of our mind? Maybe the design behind how things appear to operate in nature?

It certainly seems to be a way of learning, so I suggest you try the following ...

Thought experiment

Take a short bit of writing. It could be a poem or just some prose. Take a short phrase from it and repeat it three times, then move onto the next section and repeat it.

Once you have three of those phrases, put them together and repeat them three times.

Starting another section, repeat the process. Leave it for a while and then return to check how much you can remember.

Go through the process as revision, leave it for a while, and then come back and learn a new section as outlined above.

Notice how quickly you learn.

Hustle, magic, music, and create

"Without deviation from the norm, progress is not possible."
- Frank Zappa

Is the only way to find yourself as a musician to throw caution to the wind and get out there and hustle?

When I started in music, somebody told me that it was ridiculous to think that I could make money as a musician. But now we have courses on it, as if there is a career path. Music does not have a career path; it is more like that of the entrepreneur or gambler, the risk-taker, the chancer.

How is it taught in college? Here is how you write a hit song! Rubbish. You might be able to *analyse* a hit song and recreate something like it, but what about the anomalies, which are legion in music and art? They not only break the rules, but they are so frequent that they *are* the rule.

The viewpoint in the non-Western world is that reality can be changed radically by some form of intervention that bends or breaks the way the world works. For our thought experiment, let us agree that most of the world thinks like this, and it is us who are out of step.

Now, let us ask a simple question: are we as artists limited by rational thinking? I would say that we are. It is in the word 'ration'; after all, we do not say let us think abundantly. I would also ask: are people practical and functional in non-Western countries? The answer to that is also yes, whether you agree or not with their beliefs. So why do they believe in something that, to the rational mind, does not work?

I would suggest that it does work, whether it is real or not. What limits us in the West is what we believe to be possible. If we think something is not possible, we cast a spell on ourselves. If we think something is possible, it can lead to a change in probability, and that is why we need to hustle, to nudge probability in a positive direction. This is also one of the fundamental ideas of 'chaos magic'. Look for the small victories that encourage strange synchronicities, like the call you sensed was coming or the person you met by chance at exactly the right time. These are the true aspects of 'magical thinking', instead of what we usually think it is, such as winning the lottery by wishing for it.

We as artists need those breaks, just like the gambler and the entrepreneur, so think radically, look for opportunity, and do something strange that courts that possibility.

Thought experiment

Do something that you believe in or something that you could at least temporarily invest belief in. For instance, if you have a favourite artist, living or dead, ask them for help. Sit down in a relaxed state, imagine that they are sitting with you, ask them, and listen to what comes back. The response may come as a feeling and not something that you literally 'hear'. It could also happen over several days, and this is often how these things show up. Weird synchronicities, like turning the radio on and hearing, by chance, a programme about this particular artist. Something said will be the answer to your question. Be open to all possibilities.

You can contact someone who is a character in a song, like Ziggy Stardust. It worked for Bowie!

If you resonate with the Vikings, call on their deities. Maybe use runes to draw out an intention or outcome, making a 'sigil' to represent it. Think of the symbol Led Zeppelin used on the cover of their fourth album or the one that Prince used (you know, the one he had made as a guitar).

If you want to go deeper, have a look at the Sergeant Pepper album and check out the people in the collage. Find the mystics and magicians in there and read up on them.

Ladies and gentlemen, I give you the circus of the unreal. Let us leave the desert of the real behind and let us create by changing our minds.

Everyone loves a fool

My words are so confused
Caught in the gate while leaving you
I see you laughing through your windowpane
As I walk down Autumn Road again
Everyone loves a fool
Everyone except for you
You used to laugh at me
But left me with such misery
And I can't dance the way he can
But that doesn't make me a lesser man
Everyone loves a fool
Everyone except for you
My hand lives a lie of its own
It refuses to ask you home
The words simply will not flow
They tear the paper
I don't want you to know
I think I will go and end it all
Cause I am joker that you made a fool
There's only so much my heart can take
When all around it begins to break
Everyone loves a fool
Everyone except for you

These are the lyrics for a song that became a map to my life as it unfolded in bizarre ways.

I wrote the number for my band Red Touch before I started working with Geoff Moore, and it became a number in our set. I tell the story of how it was picked up by George Michael later in the book. After the Geoff Moore project came to an end, I carried on singing it.

The strange thing was that over the years the song's elements started to happen to me, and it was only one of several songs that my life started to emulate. As I came to awareness of this, more evidence of the effect that these creations made in my life became clear.

This experience made me realise that life copies art. How does this happen? What did I miss in all this? I started to look into this effect and experiment with it, and - like all explorations in the arts - the questions I asked were answered with yet more questions. These questions went deeper still and exposed reality to be malleable in ways that I would like to share as an artist.

I have tested out my ideas with others in songwriting groups, using NLP techniques and magical systems borrowed from around the world, and the results have been terrific.

Even if the songs do not work magically, they might be better songs with soul and impact.

Thought experiment

Hold the thought that what you create is alchemy and that it changes you as it is birthed into the world. Children also do this; they change you as well as expressing themselves. The creation of a song will likewise change you, and your task is defining that change and giving it *direction*. This is not the same as giving it a *destination,* because that would limit its potential.

So let us start with a simple rhythm, to which you can add a melody if you wish. Write it out and stick it on the wall. Sing, chant, or say the words as many times as you can over the course of a week.

Pay attention to what happens.

Italian women dance the Tarantella

"The musician may speak to you of the rhythm in all space, but he cannot give you the ear that arrests the rhythm nor the voice that echoes it." - Khalil Gibran

In the Greek myth of Arion and the Dolphin, Arion - the son of Poseidon, a great bard - entered a competition in Tarentum. After winning all of the contests, he put on a free concert for the townspeople.

In the Italian province of Taranto, Apulia, the bite of a locally common type of wolf spider, named 'tarantula' after the region (and not to be confused with what is commonly known as a tarantula today), was popularly believed to be highly venomous and to lead to a hysterical condition known as tarantism.

Arion improvised a song to excite the people based on the delirium caused by the spider venom, and he called it a 'Tarantella'. R. Lowe Thompson suggested that the dance was actually a survival from a 'Dianic' or 'Dionysiac' cult.

The supposedly curative or symptomatic Tarantella was danced solo by a spider bite victim. It was agitated in character, lasted for hours, even days, and featured characteristic music.

Whether it is taken from a Dionysiac rite or relates to a spider bite, the dance's form has been highly conserved, and across other cultures we may see further examples of curative dances if we look closely.

Shamanic cultures (including our own, in remote antiquity) believed that evil spirits were responsible for illness and that good spirits could help with the cure. The healer visited the other world by going into a trance, and in many such cultures today, this is still undertaken through music and ecstatic dance.

Our friend Christianity managed to eliminate these practices, but remnants remain in the Tarantella, and the dances of the Gypsy and Irish peoples hold similar magical connections. Irish folklore constantly references the Fae, and the music and bewitching nature of Gypsy dance is still celebrated in opera and literature.

Thought experiment

Let us look at other ecstatic dance forms: rave, disco, five rhythms. Watch any footage of music concerts.

We are the same creatures as our ancestors, dancing for the harvest, the hunt, or for battle. We have just lost the magical intention.

Track 12.

LONELY HEARTS, REPAIRED

A half-heard thing, George?

"You are far
When I could have been your star
You listened to people
Who scared you to death and from my heart
Strange that you were strong enough
To even make a start
But you'll never find peace of mind
'Til you listen to your heart"
- George Michael ('Kissing a Fool')

Nearly thirty years ago, I was involved in a project with Roger Moore's son Geoffrey. My band Red Touch was seconded into the project, with a few people being replaced, primarily for political reasons. The band was good, but somewhat at odds with the zeitgeist of the time, what with two guys with funny hairdos playing keyboards.

It was during this period that I honed my writing skills, and a handful of the numbers that I created I still play, as they were (and remain) pretty reasonable. This, I believe, was due to the focus of a project backed by management and with record company interest. Being paid to write songs is a good motivator.

I got on well with Geoff, and he used to come over to my little cottage in Kent for tea, bringing his then-girlfriend. My daughters were very young then, and I think it was all a bit beyond them, but they loved to see him and Marie Chantelle (who is now married to the Prince of Greece[11]). Geoff knew loads of celebrities, from Frank Sinatra to Elizabeth Taylor, Michael Caine to Jack Nicholson, and he also knew George Michael.

The experience was rather bizarre. We got to see how the other half lived; they were jetting about the world, having a great time, while the rest of us were skint. One of the strangest events occurred after Geoff took some of our recordings to a party at which George Michael was in attendance. The songs included one entitled 'Everyone Loves a Fool', a jazzy ballad that I wrote for Geoff and which showed off his vocal skills as a crooner.

The band was to run into problems after Geoff was taken ill after the Christmas period. He ended up in a Beverly Hills hospital, and it all started to unravel after that. An interview with Geoff's father in a national newspaper revealed that Geoff had a drug problem. Roger was reported as saying that Geoff's drug problems were due to the band, which was a surprise for the rest of us as we couldn't afford drugs, even if we'd wanted them!

However, this is what happened. About a year later, George Michael released 'Kissing a Fool'. It was very similar to my number - a jazz ballad in a similar tempo, with a similar groove, and virtually the same title. But what interested me was an interview with George in which he discussed the song and how it had come about; apparently,

_____

11 Yes, there is a prince of Greece.

the song had popped into his head while he was on a flight to America.

Of course, those of you who practice NLP will know that half-heard things have the power to manifest as 'your idea' as they pop out of your unconscious mind, and I think this is what happened in this case. I did not press the copyright issue for various reasons, and I took it as a compliment that one of my songs could do that. I do not claim that they are identical, and I do think that it was done deliberately. Many more recent copyright issues, such as Sam Smith's copying of the Tom Petty song, could also be classified in the same bracket.

George Michael died in 2016, adding to the very long list of musicians and artists who died that year. All I hope is that the Grim Reaper now turns his attention to corrupt politicians, and maybe this wish could be picked up as a half-heard thing.

Looking at how an idea can evolve and travel from a penniless musician into the head of one of the most successful artists of his time makes me contemplate how works of art have agency in the world. They are their own being. The idea that is not fully recognised by the conscious mind can slip under the radar into the unconscious, unrecognised.

You can use this as a powerful creative tool. If you want to write a piece of music in a particular style or genre, listen to that type of music while you're doing something else, so that it influences you without you being aware.

I have used this for jazzing up my own playing, putting on some Coltrane or Miles and letting it seep into my bones for a while before picking up the guitar and jamming the ideas that I have in my head.

If you can, you should

"If you can, you should reflect on the attitude of a privileged culture about choice." - Stephen Jenkinson

A friend of mine, who is a herbalist and researcher, explained how the physicians of old got into bleeding and surgery. The physicians were men trained in those skills through university or through some form of tutorship. He explained how many ailments could be treated simply and cheaply with herbs available from the village's wise women (those who had not been denounced as witches and murdered, that is).

However, if you are paying top money for a physician, then they cannot be seen to be doing what the old wives would do; they would have to dress it up as something far more complex. The history of medicine is fascinating, as this sort of thinking still holds sway. For instance, many illnesses can be cured simply through fasting and diet change, but we are programmed to think that we need an expensive expert to tell us what to do. When the cure for scurvy was discovered, one doctor said that it could not possibly be that simple.

There is an exciting similarity when it comes to music and learning, and business opportunities, if we apply the same thinking.

Firstly, do you need a teacher? Maybe so. You get off to a good start and you certainly could use some early reference points when learning a new musical instrument. If not, you can, with some focused searching, make a start more cheaply. Secondly, do you need to go to college? Think carefully. I would say that, for the network of contacts at least, maybe you do, but not in relation to the training alone. What will the qualification give you? If you want to become a teacher and a lecturer, maybe it is a good idea because the system is self-perpetuating, i.e., if you go to college, you can get the qualification you need to teach at a college.

Now consider the opening quotation: "If you can, you should." This thought is one of the driving forces behind much of what we see today. If you can afford a new phone, you should get one. If you can go to music college, you should. If you can have chemotherapy for your condition, you should.

In the past, it was much more a case of: if you can do nothing then maybe that would be best. Or perhaps it would be better stated as, "If you can do nothing, then you should do nothing."

Let me explain. We are often taught about catching things early. Most times, the body can deal with things that you never knew were a problem, and your body has been repairing itself every moment of every day since you were born. Sometimes you just need a good rest, but that is another subject.

We know that these changes happened. The words that previously encapsulated the English equivalent of the Spanish 'mañana' have fallen out of our vocabulary. We once had words for "do something tomorrow, leave it for today", but thanks to the Protestant work ethic, the Industrial Revolution, and then modern media, urging us to conform, they are long gone.

The standard business approach is to simply go with what people expect, and we see it in everything from the health industry to self-improvement, whether it be an App that helps you run a marathon with Mo Farah or get into shape with Joe Wicks.

We as artists need to think subversively, otherwise what the hell are we doing this for? If you want to make money, you should be working in the city, not playing the guitar or the drums, and if you wish for stardom, you either need something to say or to be so pretty that people become interested in listening to you.

The idea of going to music college, Brit school, BIMM, or anywhere else is maybe just a case of "If you can, you should", but now you can do this online for considerably less money, and you can even get a qualification. You need to be known, so have something to say that answers or gives voice to the questions being asked in the world.

Become creative about developing your skills. The information is out there for less cost. Go deep but not so broad in the area you are interested in. Meet people and connect. Subvert the system.

Guard against being a slave to words

"Guard against being a slave to words" – Carl Jung (The Red Book)

Rational thinking has led us to believe that words are simply labels, but as soon as we detach ourselves from that type of belief, they regain their magical potency.

Many myths and religious texts refer to the potency of words. Things spoken into being, spells being cast by cosmic deities, "In the beginning was the word". We can label something with the sound that gives us power over it. When something has a name, we can express it. We can tell others about it, think about it, and do something about it.

Without a word in a language that names or encapsulates something, we will find it hard to express anything about it. We can trace the unconscious meanings of words by looking back into their etymology. The unconscious speaks through a word's history, even when it has changed its meaning over time; it can and does cast a shadow or a spell over our reality. Words are powerful, alive, and tell us much about the culture from which they originate.

The problem with a rational knowledge of words and language is that we have lost control of the understanding of their deep structure. A genie has been let out of the bottle and now manages our thinking.

Words are indeed loaded, and as people listen to a word, they will load it with significant meanings. If you understand what is going on in somebody's mind, you can make them feel those emotions by using trigger words with intention. That is how neuro-linguistic programming works.

Rhetoric is an ancient form of using language to be persuasive and change minds and was once the whole idea behind oratory.

Let us stand and look at that from our modern viewpoint. We cannot explain how great and terrible orators such as Elizabeth I, Winston Churchill, Adolf Hitler, Charles Dickens. and Mao Zedong managed to capture people's attention and make them think differently. In Elizabeth's case, her rhetorical ability literally saved her neck. In the case of Winston Churchill, he possibly saved ours.

So don't be slaves to words; otherwise, you will be following those who have mastery of them. Instead, spend time using words thoughtfully, so that *you* get what you want. Even doing something as simple as choosing positive words over negative ones is a good start. So 'unwell' is better than 'ill', 'not so good' is better than 'bad', 'not so relaxed' is better than 'nervous'.

Words are tools of power. They are spells to be cast and worlds to be created. They are gems released from your mouth. Think of calling the world into being through your words, just like the ancient myths that were told to you: "In the beginning was the word".

I would suggest that you get some books about NLP - even the 'idiot's guide' will do (which of course is a terrible title, as you will realise by the time you get to the end of your NLP training!) - then start writing some songs that use words crafted to not just express but actually manifest the outcomes that you want.

Thought experiment

Your words create a new world every moment. Be completely aware of what you are saying and the implications that your choice of words have. Use positive words as frequently as possible, answer people in a positive tonality, and wish people well as much as possible. Pay careful attention to the effect that this has upon you and the people who listen to you. It's not so easy at first, and there will be moments where your language will not be as good as you would like it to be. Use these opportunities to rephrase and reframe what you are saying, so the next time you have the chance to speak, your language will be even more eloquent.

Think of your words now as special tools, handed down from loving ancestors. Tools that you will look after and repair, because sometimes they were misused in the past.

It may also help to have a little notebook, similar to the book of prayers or psalters that people would have carried with them in the past. It will become a collection of words and phrases that you will use at some point in the day, which you have crafted beforehand. They could be words from a song that you have written that you will use in your everyday life, magnifying their power.

Ripples in a pool

I took a small stone and turned to one of the children and said, "I'm going to show you something of how the universe works. In fact, it is most definitely how nature works."

I threw the stone into the water, and we watched the ripples radiate out. "You see the waves caused by something that is not the same as the ripples; the action itself is not the same as the effect of that action. It is essential to notice it, and, if you look, you can see it everywhere."

"The bee, when it is feeding, doesn't know that it's pollinating a plant. The benefit that it brings to all life is not his actual intention, which is true of most things. The skill is to work out what effect you can have in the world by doing something completely different. And that, my dear, is magic."

I have been fascinated by the unexpected consequences and situations when something is happening but it is challenging to work out the causative effect.

Why is it, for instance, that some people, with the same amount of practice, can learn much quicker than others, but then slow down?

How can some people learn slowly and suddenly become very good, almost overnight, for no apparent reason? I have seen this over and over again. I have had numerous experiences where somebody who could not sing, who was struggling to pitch a note and was making slow progress, turned up one day to a lesson, and suddenly this fantastic voice came out.

Remember that progress is often not linear. Progress has more of a framework of revelation, with tipping point events. I have mentioned this before, and this time I want to look at what we can do to create change indirectly.

I have long been interested in the work of Edward de Bono, who coined the term 'lateral thinking'. There are many examples, in his numerous books on the subject, of stimulating thought by coming at it laterally. For example, an American museum seeking additional funding used a dictionary as a reference source. At random, the staff chose words from the dictionary and brainstormed what it made them think of. One word that was chosen was 'mattress', which led to the museum organising sleepovers in the museum, children's parties, overnight business conferences, etc. These popular events increased the museum's funds, which led not only to their financial survival but also to a couple of Hollywood films, such as *Night in the Museum* (I'm joking - I don't know whether that's true or not!).

Sometimes we see this in our own life. A situation that may have been unpleasant can lead to an improvement in one's circumstances; a fulcrum point that creates leverage for positive change. The event and its outcome are not the same, but they are linked.

Create opportunities for things to happen. Another example is the idea explored in the book *The Dice Man,* in which decisions are based on the throw of dice. I have already mentioned Bowie and Brian Eno's use of cards (in their case, the 'Oblique Strategy' cards that Eno created). Eno was also a collector of Tarot decks, and therefore I assume that the strategy cards he created were an extension of that process.

Tarot is full of archetypal imagery that can be used in the process of songwriting and storytelling. Tarot reading at its best is storytelling; it flows and provides deeper meanings that can be missed by the reader as they fall into the storyteller trance. No longer do the features and explanations of the 'little white book' (the pamphlet that usually accompanies the cards) need to be referred to; it is all about what the reader sees on the card and its relation to the others around it. So my advice is that if it worked for Eno and Bowie, it is well worth considering for yourself.

Let's look at creating change in our own work. Use dice or cards to tell you what to do, perhaps from a list of ideas, such as starting a new hobby. Whatever the divination method tells you to do, do that. Throw yourself into learning about a new pastime, such as doing a jigsaw puzzle. See how it changes your ability to spot pieces and how your brain creates new ways of working. Then see if this affects your work.

I used jigsaw puzzles to help with spotting opportunities, and I learnt very quickly that when I got stuck, the best thing to do was to walk away. Later, when I returned with 'fresh eyes', I would spot what I could not see before.

But what about ritualistic behaviour? Of course we do this all the time: cleaning our teeth; who gets to use the bathroom first in the morning; how we order our lives. These patterns are the same, day in, day out, so let's create some that cause positive change.

Religious ritual often includes sympathetic magic, in which a symbolic representation, such as a picture of a deity or a statue of a saint, allows us to make contact with something 'other', such as the deity or saint. Actions such as crossing oneself connect us with those who have a relationship with crosses, or pathways, or even crossroads.

Religious rituals are often a way of illuminating a path, making the way forward clearer. Ganesha is an Elephant-headed god; what better way could there be to destroy roadblocks on the way ahead than by invoking him!

Do things that might provide a kickback to what you want; for instance, helping the poor in another country could enable money to come to you in return.

I sent several CVs for job interviews and noticed an increase of new pupils for my private guitar teaching. The job interviews had nothing to do with music, but I wanted to test my theory out.

Finally, remember that I have a creative experiment available through my Patreon site, the Magical Song Writing course, where we create lyrics and music to change ourselves and our surroundings.

Grief and music

"The work now is the willingness to propose grief as a radical political alertness to life, that is not a drag, is not sad, that the power of grief deepens the capacity of being alive. It is the realisation that it is not going to last." - Steven Jenkinson

Steven Jenkinson is a profound speaker dealing with the concept of grief. He has worked with hundreds of people in the last days of their lives, dealing with their fears and thoughts. I find something compelling in his work.

Music is a way of exploring emotions that we would rather keep at a distance. Maintaining unrealised feelings can lead to problems, and, for some, this can be a way of developing their work, to explore their ideas musically with the prospect of self-healing. Music therapy is not new, but I think it is worth considering as a stress buster for professional people who would rather not go to a psychiatrist or for the individual who wants to explore their family's history of grief.

I have always found music to be a potent force for dealing with life's twists and turns. I know several people who play a musical instrument to help them 'not have another breakdown' (their words, not mine).

The idea of exploring grief and writing something about the experience - making something artistic and beautiful out of it - is a positive way of transforming shadows into something compelling. Think Leonard Cohen.

Throughout history, humanity has used music for healing and expressing grief, from wailing and keening to religious music. Music expresses sorrow, whether personal or spiritual.

In our modern times, we rarely meet death, but in the past it would have been a regular occurrence. There would have been no covering up the process of dying. It would have been a common occurrence to see the death of animals, even the death of members of one's own family, close at hand. In today's society, death has become artificially sanitised.

I'm writing this in the middle of a pandemic, and society's response to this is 'death phobic' - another term of Stephen Jenkinson's, which I think aptly describes the underlying attitude towards the virus and to death.

Jenkinson's point of view is that grief is a skill that needs to be cultivated *for our sanity*. There is no logical way of dealing with something such as grief, but it has to be something that we court and get to know. It also makes us profoundly human, and that lack of being able to grieve shows how far we have lost our humanity.

Our way of dealing with grief has always involved music. Music is a technology that allows us to communicate with the other world. We can view that world as being part of our deep unconscious, containing unknowable things that in some form instruct us in life.

Music has a profoundly spiritual aspect, and even something as banal as pop music can speak to people in its universal language. Music, like all art, does not have to be cerebral; it is often more powerful the more basic it is. I have recordings of Amazonian shaman whistling and singing while accompanied by the swishing of leaves. These songs or 'Icaros' are intoxicating, even though they are in a language I do not understand. It is a language that the medicine people say is the song of the plant.

There are Amazonian plants that have a profound effect on the mental health of people who ingest them. People with schizophrenia, depression, and many other physical ailments, including cancer, have been cured with the various brews of highly skilled and intuitive indigenous peoples.

There is now a line of thought that links the psychosomatic aspect of illness to the fight-flight mechanism that we call stress, which arguably leads to many of the West's ailments. When healing with these plants, the shaman will sing their songs as they journey with those who have come to be healed.

When you dig deep to find a song, your life experience can produce a piece of art that can heal you and the person who listens. This is a gift and a blessing.

Thought experiment

Think of a song that, although sad, is powerful and also strangely optimistic. Something like 'Blue' by Joni Mitchell is a great example. Listen to it and remember a time of sadness and loss, but use it to help you think of good things that have transpired since or maybe because of the loss.

Embed that feeling of transformation into the song so that when you listen to it, recall that feeling inside you, and if you do not feel it, IMAGINE IT.

A DATE WITH MY WIFE

Give something back that hurts a little

"Give something back that hurts a little." – Steve Martyn

Often, real change comes from life events that we would rather not have experienced. However, in this society of risk-aversion, we need to embrace things that move us beyond where we currently are. Our culture is full of legislation, attitudes, and belief systems that keeps us away from anything that could hurt us or might be uncomfortable, which leads us to stagnation.

The foods that are good for us tend not to be the tastiest and are certainly not the sweetest, which has led us to obesity and all the diseases caused by that condition, and also, strangely, to a form of malnutrition due to not consuming a wide enough range of foods. Considering that we live in an affluent society, we eat a less diverse range of foods than our ancestors.

To become a great musician or athlete, you have to put in the time, forsaking other things that may be sweeter in your life, like the diverting computer game or box set or all the partying (if you have such a life!). The hours that a good musician puts in *hurts,* just as the fact that playing the guitar for three or four hours hurts your fingers and stretches the muscles to the point of cramp, not to mention the disappointment of not getting it right.

It is a form of courtship with the spirit of music and creativity. There isn't a single plan that works in courting a prospective lover. You may know what you think you are doing, but you will not get very far unless you adapt the plan to fit the person.

If making an offering of a gift during courtship, it must be something that has value to both you and them, not something you want to be rid of. When you give something of value, it should hurt.

In the past, the great artists and players did not have anything to lose by taking a risk, because life was crap anyway, so it was worth the gamble. But from our perspective of comfortable, convenient lifestyles, these risks are not undertaken to our detriment. The reality is that death will come and get you eventually anyway, so why not take the risk?

A number of the young pupils I teach come out with remarks such as, "There will be a cure for cancer soon" (I also remember that being said when I was young) and "In 20 to 30 years, we will be travelling to Mars", etc. All this stuff is a dream to keep us going, because when we actually get to Mars, it will likely not be what we thought. It will be like it has always been, sold to the people who will be populating it, just as the Europeans that populated America were sold a dream that seemed better than the nightmare from which they were escaping. They were indentured labourers, people that were slaves, bought and sold by landowners. That is how it was done in the past, and that's how the future will play out, but this time it will be in the form of a work contract with a big multinational company.

In short, any bargain that you make requires something from you; your effort, your pain, your commitment. Learning to play a musical instrument is trading in a commodity that your unconscious understands. Maybe that little bit of pain acts as the catalyst for change, in the same way that your memory of falling off a bike as a young child stays with you throughout your life, because of the hurt. But you don't just remember the pain; you also remember what the weather was like, what you were wearing, who came to help you, and what they said. Pain reinforces memory, whereas comfort (sadly!) does not.

Think of the things that were promised to you in your life. They never quite work out to the utopian vision, yet we repeatedly fall for it. Why is that? If we looked at the complex realities, we would realise that, for anything worth having, we have to work for it and pay for it in sweat and pain. So, ladies and gentlemen, pick up your guitars and play just like you did yesterday. Get down on your knees and pray; we won't get fooled again. (The Who)

Conjuring a song

Sitting in a clean, tidy space, have an empty chair opposite you.

You have prepared the room and played the type of song you wanted to conjure as you were getting ready. The objects placed in the room are the ones that would please and maybe excite the spirit of the song.

You have lit candles that have been prepared, maybe with essential oils or a lamp with a message written on paper placed underneath.

There are libations to that spirit; whiskey for hard rock, wine for a love song, rum or Ganga for the reggae daemon. If you felt the need, you have drawn two circles, one for each chair, and - depending on how you think - written sacred or barbarous names around the edge of the circles.

Sit quietly and take some deep breaths and relax. If you have a meditation practice, do that for a short period. Perhaps you have some other way of taking you into your alpha or theta brainwaves, such as a theta metronome.

Now you are in that space, call in the spirit of the song. Play or wait in quietness. Go with your senses, lose yourself in the process. I mix the two; I play, then I listen. I might talk to the song spirit. I would suggest that you record this because the ideas might be forgotten when you land.

Invite the spirit into the empty chair and let her talk, sing, tell you stories. Let her dance through you. What happens cannot and does not need explanation. Let the flow state happen and embrace the liminal space.

When you feel it is done, let her go with a licence to depart and a request that she will visit again when you call. May your romance continue and strengthen.

Thought experiment

Listen to the Paul Simon song 'Cecilia'. Listen carefully to the lyrics and write a brief note about what you think it means. Do this before you read the next paragraph.

Now consider that Saint Cecilia is the patron saint of musicians and think about the lyrics in light of this new information.

I would suggest that it is both Paul Simon's evocation of the Saint and a reflection upon writer's block. You might not see it like that, but I do think there is something in that. And if evoking a saint is good for Paul Simon, it's probably good for us.

Trojan horse

Over years of teaching and playing music, I have come to the firm belief that it is one of the best ways for the young to develop self-confidence, to keep that creative spark, and access original thought by playing and creating music.

This bold claim is based on how creative lateral techniques, such as cut up, can generate novel ideas, unrestricted by preconceived paradigms, and my goodness, don't we need that now!

I have seen children as young as six create complex melodies and lyrics, beautiful songs with original structures, just because they could. No one was marking or standing in judgement on their works, and because of that, they were free to innovate.

I believe that if they grow up with this freedom remaining consistent, they will think differently, and maybe they will think of solutions to the problems that we have left them.

A problem is not solved by using the same thinking that caused it. This has been said by minds far more significant than mine.

The solutions to the problems of this world need new thinking that is not predicated on old paradigms.

Just before the pandemic hit, I started a charity called Ikaro Music. I had a vision for the charity to enable young children to learn music and create songs. There is a barrier to starting music even in this day and age of reasonable affluence, because parents think it might be a fad; they don't want to start lessons and buy an instrument only for their child to stop a few months later.

I've always found this a short-sighted view because the very act of learning and having an instrument around can fundamentally change how a young mind develops.

Once the charity and its advertising have created enough traction, my plan is for the songwriting techniques to be made available online for free.

I know from my own experience that with very little musical knowledge and technical expertise, children can create and then become fascinated by music and the arts. I believe this is to be a very potent force for good. However, it is also a Trojan Horse, and inside is the development of that young mind.

For all the good intentions of education, it is still based on creating a specific type of person for a particular kind of society, one which I genuinely believe is failing dismally. The contents of this course could give us an opportunity as a species to adapt and move forward to meet the challenges created from our past behaviours.

We seriously need to change the way we think and how we view the world. While there have been significant advances in the sciences to understand more fully how the mind and the brain work, that reality may not continue to exist in the way that we've always believed it does. It's more a case of the internal representation of what we experience, and this fundamentally changes our relationship with the world and our thinking. Therefore, for anything to change, we need to change our thinking

There is much that we can do with this concept of the Trojan Horse for ourselves. Changing behaviour patterns, such as changing what time we eat, what hours we spend asleep, and when we sleep. Changing our patterns of consuming social media and television, when we listen, and what we listen to is essential to the world that we construct. This knowledge means that contained within that change are new potentials; our Greek army who come out at night and unlock the gates of Troy.

Jobs and dreams

"When I was five years old, my mother always told me that happiness was the key to life. When I went to school, they asked me what I wanted to be when I grew up; I wrote down 'happy'. They told me that I did not understand the assignment, and I told them they did not understand life." – John Lennon

Happiness is playing music with others.

It seems that whenever I meet new people, and after they have asked me what I do, they tell me about a guitar that they used to play but had to stop because family and life got in the way, and now they wish they could start again.

Some of them romanticise about the times they played in a band or think about the guitar they sold, and all of them lament the fact that if they had carried on playing, they would be outstanding by now.

One sad thing in today's world is that people spend many years training to do a job, going to university, and getting into debt, only to find that the job they have secured through all that hard work is one that they actually hate.

It does not bring them any happiness; the money might be helpful, but with the increase of money coming in, there is a corresponding increase of money going out.

I teach in several public schools, and when I see the expense of the parents' lifestyles, I am amazed. Adding up the cost of two expensive cars, school fees for the children, an expensive house, expensive holidays, and the stress of a job that they do not like, they could easily afford to have a happier life. By cutting back and focusing on the things that honestly give them happiness, life would be less stressful.

I understand that once you get used to a lifestyle, and the rest of the family get used to your income, it can be very challenging to extricate yourself. Sometimes your body does it for you by making you ill if you don't heed the warnings.

So let's do something about it. Find some time to jam and have fun meeting other people. This could be through an open mic night or could just be getting together with a few friends and making a bit of noise. Think yourself back a little bit to when music gave you happiness; invoke those memories and bring some joy back into your life.

As one grows older, you begin to realise that many things we were told were lies, such as how important science and maths is, to the arts' detriment. After learning them, you never used many important subjects again, like finding the area of a rhombus or calculating the value of X and Y.

Use social media (sparingly): if you haven't got enough friends who play instruments, make new contacts by asking around. Start a band, book a gig, and have some fun.

The Interview

On an open stage, apart from two empty chairs in front of a large projection screen and a small table with a glass and some water.

Enter the interviewer and interviewee. They take their seats to rapturous applause, and as the audience quietens, the interview begins.

NN: So, here we are in this lovely theatre. Thanks for coming to talk to me about the book.

Richard E.: Wait, I should be the one greeting you! Although you actually need no introduction.

NN: But you're going to do it anyway!

Richard E.: Yeah.

NN: So ... Dr Rich, over to you!

Richard E. *(Turning slightly to face the audience)*: Yes, thanks for that. So, I've invited NN to talk to us tonight about creativity, his writing a book about it, and the process of getting it out there. *(Turning back to NN):* You've experienced such enormous success, I think there's a lot we can learn from you.

NN: Well, this is interesting because we spoke about this stuff a long time ago when we were in the process of creating it. And I think it's fascinating doing this event, now that we've been successful with it. I didn't know it would be such a big hit when I talked to you back then.

I was doing this because I thought the story needed to get out there. It's all about people reconnecting to their creativity and what that means. I think I told you the story, didn't I? About the single I did when I was in my 20s? We had a few of the records we made sent off to radio stations, and we started to get airplay, although we didn't even know it was happening at first.

The BBC picked it up. Just a local station, but they came out and recorded us in concert and paid us for it. And the odd thing was that the payment was almost exactly the same as the single had cost us to record and press. It was so bizarre, I can remember the band sitting around thinking, "This is nuts!"

So we could just have taken all these records and given them away and we would have got our money back. That episode has stayed with me all my life, through 40 years of experience. And you know, the book has followed the same principle.

I asked myself some simple questions: what does this book do? What solutions does it have for peoples' problems?

Then I thought of a 'road opener'. Now, I know you know about road openers, but for the people sitting in the audience who don't ... I mean, you've done stuff with road opening, haven't you?

Richard E.: Yes, a little. An example that leaps to mind was my first trip abroad after the lockdown was lifted and it became possible to travel again. Everything was stacked against you; if you wanted to go abroad, you had to have umpteen pieces of paper; everyone was very stressed. You had a short window of time in which you had to get yourself PCR tested, get the result back, and so on. Do you remember it? What a nightmare those days were. That was when I really upped my game in terms of talking to Ganesha.

NN: Yes, Ganesha! For those who don't know, Ganesha

is the elephant-headed Hindu deity, who - along with an elephant's head - has a broken tusk. It looks like a bit of a mess, but loveable. It's a truly benevolent being, and, of course, if you want to open a road and get rid of the obstacles that stand in your path, what better way than having an elephant to help with the heavy lifting? It's a concept that appears in every culture; a spirit that moves obstacles, focusing on the benefits of the adherents.

Rich E: Yes.

NN: This project is not really about me, and I'm not banging my drum here. It was really to get people to find their own drum and start hitting it. Once people realise how this stuff works and connects to you as a person, as a being, then it becomes something more than just, "I'm going to sit down and write a song." If you sit down and write a song or a poem in these ways, it's going to unlock you. That part that connects with everything else. It sounds incredibly grand, but I mean it.

Richard E.: Yeah.

NN: And I, you know... as with your experience of travelling, I'm sure you noticed that things started to click.

Richard E.: Yeah, once you become aware, the synchronicities are crazy. In my case, the number 23 kept coming up, which is 'Splitting Apart' in the IChing. That number kept coming up on the journey, and everything went smoothly. But really, all I'd done was - rather than spend time worrying - thinking ahead to enjoying being at our destination and repeating a mantra to Ganesha: "Om Gam Ganapataye Namaha." He's a joyful entity, as you know, and he wants in. He likes the thrill of it. He wants to be invoked.

The screen at the back comes to life, and the form of Ganesha appears. It morphs into a statue in a temple where a young woman brings a bowl of milk and puts it at the god's feet.

Richard E.: One of the things we should talk about is that bit that comes after the creative phase of writing a book about songwriting. When you've got it over the line, at least in the sense that you feel like "This is now done". And, traditionally, something I would typically do at this point is sort of collapse in a heap, exhausted. But really, the work then is only beginning. You have to get it out there.

NN: Yeah, and that is the tricky bit.

Richard E.: Yeah.

NN: I'm probably going to contradict myself here several times, but creativity and marketing are not the same. When you come up with creative ideas, you don't want to edit until it's time to edit. It's the same with marketing; when you're creating the thing, you don't want to create it in such a way that you're thinking about selling it. When you get to the point of selling, you are not making anymore, you are selling, and selling can be a creative process as well, though it's different. Very different.

Richard E.: Yes, this is what I wanted to get into. Go on.

NN: So, creativity is the selling of it. It is about finding demand … you are uncovering the desire that somebody has for the thing that you've produced. That element has been there from the very beginning because you saw a gap in the market for your creation.

So, in its way, marketing is another form of creativity, which is, of course, where the character, like Hermes or Mercury, the great salesman, comes in. They are the ones who can talk the hind leg off a donkey! They are the characters who can steal something from somebody and sell it back to them, which is precisely Hermes' story. At the very beginning, we see Hermes take Apollo's cattle and get away with it, effectively selling the idea back to Apollo.

So you're looking for the way you can hang it on the person. That is probably not the right word ... I mean the desire that that person has for the thing that you have.

What is it that people need? If you take yourself back, and we haven't got out of this situation as such, to the 'golden era' of almost everybody having more ready money for things, there was an attitude where everybody thought it would just carry on - you know, ecology and the economy - it was something somehow separate from them.

Then, as this book was coming out, the shit hit the fan. At that point, it became expensive to travel, to do anything, to heat your house and buy fuel. All of that, cutting in that point, was almost perfect timing for the book. Suddenly, you're going to have to think differently. You can't just do what people did before, because it will not be enough.

I was interested in this process because the charity had also gone from strength to strength. We needed different ways of thinking, requiring a completely different paradigm, and we didn't know what it was.

Creativity is the thing that gives us a different paradigm. It has to form its own way, and it's going to come from young people, if they're not burdened with the education system. That's the point: if we can keep the doorways open, then they may think differently.

So, in a nutshell, what I did was contact all the people

who knew me through my lessons, group teaching, the podcast, the summer schools, and the gigs. Then I started to leverage those connections, and I really ratcheted up the cache of what I did and how I got my ideas across to generate interest.

The great thinker Bob Proctor came up with the idea that, if you had a book, you are now an authority, and it's true even in these days. Forgetting that I've been doing this all my life, and I have taught lots and lots of very well-known players, as soon as that book was out it made a difference.

Going along with the idea I expressed about the single: we gave away a lot of books, but each one of those opened a doorway to funding for the charity and an incredible amount of coverage that I could never have paid for. That in turn gave me extra teaching work, which helped build revenue and enabled me to promote the book even further. So that was the process.

The book is now used in education and in schools, and its involvement in a university in London also made a big difference. Some people were quite puzzled, obviously, because of the use of magical thinking, but then it became abundantly clear to them that this stuff was already going on with the great artists, and I quote a lot of them in the book. So, by default, this stuff must work.

Richard E.: Yeah, I think one of the most gratifying things about the book's success has been the fact that it's been adopted, kind of secretly, within the education system, by the more free-thinking, maverick teachers. Many of your creative techniques are pure magic, but, by being taken on board as innovative teaching techniques, they slipped under the radar.

You can see the benefits: the emergence of new cultural opportunities, mainly localised community-based ones, for young people to get involved, be creative, overcome their feelings of limitation, and overcome the emerging economic downturn.

The picture of Ganesha on the screen seems to smile at the audience.

NN: Exactly. My initial idea was, as you know, to teach the teachers to lead in this way. But of course, because it changes so quickly, technology has already disempowered email. What I mean by this is that people weren't reading most of their emails anymore. If you're in a school, you're not interested in an email from an unknown person, it's just more spam. It was being screened out by the schools; they didn't know who I was. So even at that point, email wasn't going to cut it. I realised that I had to sort of go back to analogue. I had to get a couple of schools to start and network their ideas for the schools to communicate with one another and say, "This is amazing - we've got these kids doing stuff and they've got some belief in themselves developing." Even though they haven't got money and haven't necessarily got the advantage of a family life that gives them the capacity to think differently. As I told the schools where I started doing this stuff, it's really a Trojan horse.

What you've got on the surface is that they're going to learn to play the guitar and write a song. The Trojan horse element is that they've suddenly got this ability to create, not learn, and I'm not giving them anything other than permission to use the skills they already had. Their imagination to think differently. They can put it on paper and play with it, which is a magical process. You can take something, which could be somebody else's idea, and use it as 'materia magica'. You've cut it in such a way and juxtaposed it with something else, and it's yours now.

Richard E.: Yeah.

The screen shows a large tree full of acorns. The picture pans out to show a forest of trees with lots of oaks, full of wildlife.

NN: It's like taking an acorn off a tree and taking some water from a spring, taking a feather you found in a particular spot - which might have been a place a Saint has been - and you have a relationship. You build a relationship with something. Then, you know, that relationship can be with your guitar. That relationship can be with your ability to write a particular type of poem, a sonnet if you like. I'm not saying it could be a form. It can be a dance or it could be a form of sport. It could be, you know, the way that you do your gardening. The Japanese have got this nailed; this idea that you garden so that you can discover yourself. You can sweep the path in a way that makes you find enlightenment. I'm looking at this from that point of view.

It doesn't get all the correct answers, but it doesn't matter. For many people, it is a bit of a mind blaster. I know you like to use the term 'shit wizard' for yourself, but it's that idea; you're still a wizard.

Richard E.: Yep, standing up here for shit wizards everywhere.

NN: Exactly, and everybody's a shit wizard. If you read about Crowley's life, many things didn't work out the way he expected.

Richard E.: Yeah, behind the sensational headlines. Obviously, he did as much as anyone to cultivate those because he liked the attention, but he went from a psychological view of magic to one where he thought, "Actually, maybe there is something external out there."

NN: Yes, because there's a whole bunch of stuff going on here that we seem to have no control over.

Richard E.: Yeah. I was going to say that, in addition to the book being adopted in a school setting, lots of anecdotal accounts started to come through from people of all ages and backgrounds. These people had felt that they had nothing creative within them - they were a frustrated guitarist or drummer, or they'd done something in the past but failed to pick it up again - and you enabled them to have a go. You say it throughout the book: "Try it, stop thinking about it, and get on with it."

The repetition of that and the techniques you've provided allowed a lot of people to overcome feelings of social isolation, which has been increasing, and step outside the firehose of media propaganda coming through all the regular channels and online streaming services. Get away from the isolation and the binary thinking that fuels the dystopian visions of the box sets on the streaming platforms and get back to finding yourself.

NN: See, that's the thing. You need to come from the perspective that maybe every animal living on Earth does what the bee does. Its primary ecological function is unknown to the bees themselves. It's just trying to get something to eat and return to the safety of the hive, but in the process of doing that it creates all of life by pollinating plants. The bee doesn't know that. And maybe that is the function of many creatures, including us. Our thoughts and beliefs about who we are and what we believe in may create the world of the spirits. It makes gods. They didn't exist because we weren't there at that time. But as soon as we started to be there, they lived; we created something beyond.

Richard E.: If I may jump in on that one, I think they were there already. But when we came along; we became the bees that supported the ecosystem.

NN: Yes, that gave them their food.

Richard E.: Yeah.

NN: One idea is that if you don't keep on honouring gods and giving them offerings, they die. That is a theme of Neil Gaiman, and I think it sounds plausible.

Richard E.: Yeah, it's all about co-creation.

NN: And we don't know and can never know. This is the part of the book where I discuss that we are part of the creative process when we write a song, but we are not the one who writes the song; we are just part of it. When you realise that, it means we are doing something divine. It's something beyond what we are. Just as the bee is doing something beyond what it is. At the very least, it says we shouldn't spend our time wallowing in the muck of negativity.

Satish Kumar, when I interviewed him, said, "If you want peace, focus on peace." Peace is not an absence of war; it's something different. When you create, you create the thing you want in the world, and you are part of that process and the steering of that process. The energy that you're using is amoral. It's not good or bad, it's just a thing.

And you can do all this stuff with it. You steer it. Just like when you work with the land to improve the land and produce good things - you can nudge nature in the way that it's going to work, right? Which is permaculture, right?

Richard E.: Yes. Like when people realise that they don't want to watch something negative because they don't want that in their world.

Vic H: You need to shake the system up now and again. Because that's how life is; you need something that rocks the boat now and again because that's how nature works. So, now and again, you get drunk and watch a terrible film that makes you feel miserable to rock the system, and then you get back into it again. So it's not a case that you should never do that, it's a case of understanding it. It's all part of the way that creation works.

Richard E.: Yeah, you have to have an occasional brush with your shadow and the shadow of the world.

NN: Yeah, absolutely.

Richard E.: And it's hard to avoid anyway. Dipping in and out of the dystopia.

NN: Yes, but it is a case of dipping in and out of it. That's the point.

Richard E.: Yes, in and out.

NN: So, yeah, I've been excited about what's happened with this book, beyond what I expected. In a way, I didn't think too much about it. It's often best not to have a plan or think about it too much, though it goes against the New Aeon method of writing down exactly what you want. It's better to open up the thing and maybe have a vision of what could happen.

Richard E.: What could happen?

NN: The result. Instead of telling people exactly what you want.

Richard E.: Yeah, I think that's true, and important. There's the point where you're thinking about yourself in the future, experiencing the success of the creative endeavour, and you don't want to think about how you get there. There is a point in the process where you're doing the editing, and then you've got to do those steps that get it out there, and you want to do that so that you're focusing enough that it actually happens. But also, you're keeping your options open, because the more possibilities there are for it to succeed, the more likely it is that one of those will bear fruit. Can you talk about that a little bit, the balance?

NN: Yeah, because it's pretty tricky.

Richard E.: Yeah, true. In truth, I asked you the question because I don't know the answer.

NN: Yeah, I wonder what it is. I'll give you an example from real life. My life. I did a ritual to ask for a certain amount of money to get me through a particular problem, settle everything down, and all the rest.

I worked with a spirit. I won't say who it was, but it was one of the demons that you can petition for money. I got virtually the exact amount that I asked for, but - as it turned out - in order to get it, I had to have a heart attack and a stroke. So they were absolutely right; they got me what I asked for but took it down a route that was the easiest way to get it. Now, in hindsight, it would have been better to say, "I see myself doing this" and explain the scenario where you're in a particular place, doing specific things, and you've got a certain type of house and all the rest of it. And just literally open it up to possibilities.

Richard E.: Yes.

NN: You hear this from others; you get what you ask for but not necessarily the way you expected it. So, when I looked at the book, I decided to talk to people about where it will be. For example, here we are in this lovely theatre with an audience listening to us rabbit on about the stuff we are interested in and what we did with the book. On a national TV programme about the arts. I mean, I would never have thought of that, but I imagined it as a future possibility.

If you told someone this, they would think this was …

Richard E.: … the delusional ramblings of a madman?

NN: Exactly, or two mad men, as it turns out. And, in this process, you've also managed to become well-known in your own right.

I think it is essential that people take magical thinking seriously now.

It was always happening in the background. Some great thinkers have been talking about magic, chipping away at this stuff: Jason Miller, Aidan Wachter, The Scarlets, Alex Cummings, Duncan Barford and Alan Chapman, Gordon White. These people are brilliantly clever, and they mix magic into their lives as artists, writers, and academics.

What I try to do with the book is to say, look, the icons in pop music, Bowie, Lennon, Cobain, and the Stones, they're all doing it, so you gotta do it. That's what it's about.

Richard E.: Yeah.

NN: Instead of just thinking, "It's cheating" … if that's cheating, then the Beatles and Led Zeppelin were cheating. And, you know, they were all cheating.

Richard E.: Yeah, and cheating who exactly?

NN: Well, cheating the establishment that thinks that you've got to go college and spend a lot of time learning and paying somebody a lot of money to learn a lot of stuff, which is out of date. That's the point. You don't have to spend a lot of money studying this stuff. Just go and damn well do it. Sure, if you think, "I want to go and see this person and pay them to show me the essence of what they do", then great. I'm not saying, "Don't do it", just ignore the establishment telling you that you can't do the thing without the piece of paper that says you can do it.

I've spent enough years examining for colleges. It's getting that balance right of having goals and discovering who you are, because that's the thing: find out who you are.

The screen brings up a picture of the book cover. As the book opens, lights flash out from the pages into the audience.

Richard E.: Yeah, exactly. You talk about this in the book, that ultimately you have to do it for yourself, experience it, and embody what works for you, and it will inspire you to develop your creative practice.

And that was the advice that really kicked everything off. Many of the anecdotes that came back weren't just, "Oh, I did what you said in the book". It was much more like, "How about this thing that happened!" We learnt from our readership a whole bunch more stuff that we had not known before.

NN: Yeah, totally. The things that I love are weird. The weird stuff like, "This happened and then that happened, and then that happened. What the hell's going on?"

That's how the world works. It talks to you.

Richard E.: Yeah.

NN: It's like the story I shared with you a few times about the Teddy Bear incident. This is not in the book, but I was followed around by a teddy bear once. I'd watched the film Ted, the first one and then the second one. Then I was listening to a podcast while I was driving, and they were talking about a bear haunting the Tower of London. Back in the 1870s, this guard in the Tower of London sees a bear coming out at him, and he goes at it with his bayonet, and because it's a ghost, it goes straight through the bear and ends up in the door. And as I'm listening to this, I come around the corner of my road, and this guy at the end of my road has a giant teddy bear leaning against his gate. And it's like, "OK, this is telling me something. But I have no idea what."

And then I started looking for a room to rent. My life was falling apart at this time, and I turned up at this shambling manor house, a 12th Century manor house with a moat. I walk into the kitchen and it's like nothing's been done to it since the 1970s. Seriously, maybe a cooker went in there about 1990, right? And I walked into the corridor, and the ceiling had come down! And I went into the room they were letting, and it looked lovely. And in the corner is a big teddy bear looking at me. And the lady starts talking about the teddy bear. Of all the things in the room, she starts talking to me about this teddy bear; that it belongs to the daughter of the man renting it. And this teddy bear looks like Ted from the film. I don't understand what's happening here, but something is stalking me.

Richard E.: So, did you rent the room or not?

NN: No. I think it was saying to me, this place is haunted.

Richard E.: Run away!

NN: Yes.

Some pictures of mediaeval demons flash across the screen, and pictures of ink in glasses of water take the form of figures with horns and hoofed feet.

Richard E.: That brings us back to demons. I mean, demons are just doing their job, right? But they tend to be tetchy and have a sense of humour. So if you ask them for money and leave it at that ...

NN: ... they'll give you the money, but they'll have a joke with you as well.

Richard E.: Yeah, so you need to think creatively about how you engage with such things. My glib suggestion is that obtaining the money should harm none.

NN: Yes, including me!

Richard E.: Yeah. You know, I did have a similar thing. I had a problematic relationship with money because I had in mind that it was a zero-sum game. like there was a finite sum of money out there. And if I had more, someone had to have less, which caused me problems, and I had to get away from thinking that. Money is made up.

NN: Yes, it's magic.

Richard E.: And powers much greater than us, at least politically and economically, are doing this stuff. It's not down to us, and it's not a zero-sum game. And so I had to change my relationship with money. I conjured for, I don't know ... let's say 20,000 pounds. And what turned up was a bill for 20,000 pounds. Apparently there had been some error going on for years with my tax code or something. It was calamity central, but it quickly changed my relationship with money. I found that I could pay that bill within terms, and although I did it through, you know, things I'm not proud of - credit card limits, borrowing a bit here and there, and selling a few things, - it got done. It made me realise that this whole thing is fluid.

NN: Yes.

Richard E.: I came out the other side with a bunch of techniques that meant I didn't have to be as enslaved or fearful of money anymore.

NN: Yes, that is a brilliant story. Cool stuff. I think now we are done for time?

Richard E.: Yes, let's wrap it up. I enjoyed this! Should we? We could try this again.

NN: Actually, we've got another talk lined up at some point. Is it here or is it somewhere in the middle of London? I can't remember, but anyway, let's do that,

Richard E.: Yeah, alright.

NN: Yeah, we'll have to, so those in the audience who want to spend more money to hear us ramble on about something else can come and we'll sign some more books.

Richard E.: Yeah, if you enjoyed travelling in to hear us talk about magic, creativity, music, and NLP, please come again!

NN: We could do a ritual. Now, we shouldn't say that, should we? No.

Richard E.: But alright.

NN: Excellent stuff. Goodnight all.

As the two leave the stage to rousing applause, the screen flashes up a picture of Robert Anton Wilson with his trademark white goatee beard and the following quotes:

"Every dark night of the soul is followed by a golden dawn."

"Things are not all dark, it just depends on what angle you see it from."

"You are more creative if you are more optimistic."

His picture fades into a large yellow sunflower.

The Old Uncle's Library

The old be-spectacled man was sitting in the sunshine with a small cup of very strong espresso coffee. The early morning light was breaking through, with its warming rays, in the Athenian suburb where he lived. Behind him was an extensive library of books, all of which seemed to have been read on countless occasions; none were in pristine condition, all were thoroughly thumbed and marked.

The old man, a perpetual student, spent hours reading and pondering, often muttering to himself or committing lines of text to memory out loud, as if to keep back the ravages of old age.

A knock broke this morning meditation over the black espresso.

"Uncle, it's me, Stefanos. Can I come in?"

"Of course, Stefanos! Come, and share some time with your old uncle," he replied.

A young man came into the room. He was in his mid-teens and was a striking-looking lad with an air of seriousness.

"What can I do for you today, Stefanos?" asked the old man.

"Uncle, Mother has suggested that I come for some books. She believes you might be able to help me with a little project."

"Of course, my boy. You know, I've probably got the very book you need. So, what is it you are studying?"

Stefanos looked around the room at all the books. "I've been interested in some of the old stories from a psychological point of view. I was curious to know more about how the ancients considered creativity."

"Now that's interesting, because I have many stories I could share with you. It depends on what you want to know, because maybe the ancients didn't consider creativity in the way that we do, or even the idea of psychology."

"How so?" asked Stefanos.

"Because the ancients considered creativity as a gift from the gods, or assistance from a spirit of nature. In fact, the past was infused with so much magic, we would find it very difficult to understand without putting the magic back in."

The young man eyed his old uncle with suspicion.

Even though Stefanos called him Uncle, the man was much older than that, probably a great uncle or even maybe just a friend or a great-grandparent's friend. He seemed perpetually young, and even though the years had drawn deep lines on his face, he was incredibly fit and healthy. He would take long walks every day in the beautiful sunshine, and his mind was as sharp as a tack, but the stories he told, well, nobody knew whether they were true or not. But they were truly magnificent, and that was why Stefanos was unsure whether his uncle was about to launch into one of his 'fables'.

"Well, Uncle, I need some reference books that I can refer to. It might be difficult for me to refer to your stories, if you don't mind."

The old man smiled. "Yes, OK. So where to start? Well, let's talk a little bit about books that may challenge our thinking."

He walked over to a shelf, picked up several books, and brought them to the table.

"Let's start with these, on magic. These are very easy to follow and give a personable way of thinking about and doing magic, which is excellent for someone like you who can see under the bonnet of how a system works and do your own thing once you see it in someone else's life.

"I would suggest these before any of the magical grimoires. Get some simple workings in before you look at the ancient books.

"I have always found that magic evolves with the culture that contains it. Even though the old ways are still best in the long run, sometimes it is difficult to plug back into it, as it is we who have changed. However, once strange things start happening and you begin to see that it is real ... magic, I mean ... then you can take a look at these books."

The old man took to his feet and walked over to another set of books, bringing them over to the table, reading the titles as he placed them down: "The Greek Magical Papyri, The Book of Oberon, The Hygromanteia, and The Book of St Cyprian, my namesake."

"Oh, Uncle Cyprianos, you are named after a magical Saint!"

The old man smiled. "There are many grimoires to find and read, but I would suggest you start with these, as they are what I have most treasured. But if you are interested, I can give you a list of others."

"But Uncle, you know I find all this magic stuff a bit weird."

"I know you do, Stefanos, but the secret is how we see the world without psychology but with magic. We have different explanations for the same elements. Once you have got your head around this, you will see the whole world in a richer and more connected way.

"By the time we finish, there will be so many books you won't be able to carry them out! But if I put them on the shelf over there, you can dip into them or take some out to read them in your own time."

"What about the stuff that's not weird magic. The more psychological stuff?"

"Well," said Cyprianos, "I would suggest you look at books on Neurolinguistic Programming; NLP. The approaches will also be beneficial in your own life, and there are a couple of other things that would help.

"And of course, if you look at Jung's work, particularly the Red Book, you will realise that all that area of enquiry is based on magical thinking.

"The whole era of creativity is not logical, and you may find that many artists, musicians, dancers, and poets are all involved in some form of magic, even if they don't see it that way. The idea of having a vision in your head and allowing it to unfold, dancing things into existence, and speaking them into a reality is all magic.

"I'll tell you what I'll do, my boy. I'll make a list and then I will put all the books in a particular place for you to look at, and then I'll let you work out what to look at. You might find some fascinating and others less so. Use your intuition to guide you."

"Thank you, Uncle, that is very kind," said Stefanos, and, as he got up to leave, his uncle said to him, "Is there a new woman in your life?"

"Yes, there is Uncle."

"Do you feel differently about this one?"

"Oh, she is very, very special."

"Well, that feeling, that indescribable feeling, is magic. And what is her name?"

"Justina."

The old man gave a wry smile. "I knew someone with that name once. A long, long time ago; she was a very rare beauty. Because of her, I lost my head, but we can never truly come to our senses without losing our heads."

Recommended reading

In no particular order:

- *Teach Yourself NLP* by Steve Bavister and Amanda Vickers

- *Weaving Fate* by Aidan Wachter

- *The Healing Forces of Music* by Randall McClellan, PhD

- *Wisdom of Mental Illness* by Jez Hughes

- *The Chaos Protocols* by Gordon White

- *The Elements of Eloquence* by Mark Forsyth

- *The British Book of Spells and Charms* by Graham King

- *Six Ways* by Aidan Wachter

- *Myths of the World* by Tony Allan

- *I Ching Translation* by Richard Wilhelm

- *Impro* by Keith Johnstone

- *SSOTBME* by Ramsey Dukes

- *Noise* by Jacques Attali

- *The Invisibles* by Grant Morrison

- *Mastering Witchcraft* by Paul Huson

- *Liber Kaos and Liber Null and Psychonaut* by Peter J Carroll

- *Condensed Chaos* by Phil Hine
- *A Century of Spells* by Draja Mickaharic
- *Secrets of the Talking Jaguar* by Martin Prechtel
- *Trance Formations* by Richard Bandler
- *A Life Divined* by Hamish Miller
- *Bring out the Magic in Your Mind* by Al Koran
- *The Magical Universe of William Burroughs* by Matthew Levi Stevens
- *The Red Book* by Carl Jung
- *The Cunning Man's Handbook* by Jim Baker
- *Propaganda* by Edward Bernays
- *Skin in the Game* by Nassim Taleb
- *Jerusalem* by Alan Moore
- Enjoy your reading! With love, from your Uncle Cyprianos,

So what now?

The aim of this book was to be like an absorbing trip into an old book shop or tool shed. It is now up to you to take the ideas further. Craft a creative life for yourself, write songs, or do something else that helps the unlimited possibilities that you contain to flourish, unleashed.

The book has been laid out in a cut-up style as a homage to Sgt Pepper, the Beatles, and William S Burroughs, with no direction other than what you might see. No map, other than what you can form.

Imagine what can come to you by being open, questioning what, why, and how? Use the psychological trickery within its pages to explore these possibilities.

The psychological techniques herein are really just a cipher for witchcraft, mysticism, and shamanism, whether that be Jung or NLP, and if it looked like science, it was a sleight of hand, mouth, and mind that made it so.

Science has become a religious devotion and not the process it once was. You cannot follow the science' any more than you can follow the baking or the fire-making. Science cannot tell us more than a drill can say about anything other than what a drill does.

Science can show us a process, just as alchemy could, but the clever use of words makes alchemy become chemistry. However, sitting just inside are magical practitioners like Jack Parsons; while inventing the rocket fuel that got humanity to the moon, he was also evoking the Goddess Babalon in a series of rituals in the desert.

The whole story is far weirder, more exciting and inspiring than the logical explanation, and it leads to places far more interesting.

So go and make your life magical by creating. It will change your life, your world, and your reality.

Cut up and other techniques will give you limitless possibilities to get you out of the thinking rut.

As with all things, one only needs to be consistent, doing the process frequently for it to impact on your thinking, so it's not a case of trying, but doing.

I have used these ideas for many years, with great results in my teaching of music and singing, such as with the 'Blues Camp UK' project, where the team get inexperienced amateurs to play in a band, write songs, and then perform them. Also in my work with the Ikaro Music Project charity, where young children who would not be able to afford lessons learn to play guitar and write songs over a 10-week course, with the more experienced working with me in a band playing in music venues. If those ideas work for them, they will work for you.

The education system is great for the left-side analytical aspect of the brain, but not for the right-side creative, and for us to think new thoughts and see the world as an integral ecosystem, we need that.

The system is great at entrainment, in the machine society where someone else is deemed the expert. But we are now in a time in which new ideas are needed, and each of us individually needs ideas that are not part of an echo chamber.

As The Who said, "Pick up my guitar and play, just like yesterday, and I fall on my knees and pray we won't get fooled again."

Milton Keynes UK
Ingram Content Group UK Ltd.
UKHW010920080324
439029UK00004B/274